DATE DUE

GAYLORD   PRINTED IN U.S.A.

KILLING TIME
LIFE IN THE
ARKANSAS PENITENTIARY

KILLING TIME

LIFE IN THE ARKANSAS PENITENTIARY

BRUCE JACKSON

CORNELL UNIVERSITY PRESS | ITHACA AND LONDON

Other books by Bruce Jackson:

A Thief's Primer
Wake Up Dead Man: Afro-American Worksongs from Texas Prisons
In the Life: Versions of the Criminal Experience
Get Your Ass in the Water and Swim like Me: Narrative Poetry from Black Oral Tradition
Folklore and Society (editor)
The Negro and His Folklore in Nineteenth-Century Periodicals (editor)

First published 1977 by Cornell University Press.
Published in the United Kingdom by Cornell University Press Ltd., 2–4 Brook Street, London W1Y 1AA.

International Standard Book Number 0-8014-1101-7
Library of Congress Catalog Card Number 77-6895
Printed in the United States of America
Librarians: Library of Congress cataloging information appears on the last page of the book.

This is for everyone who tried making a day in Cummins prison and in all those other iron- and wire-bounded barracks and tanks and cells.
It is for those who want them better than they are, never again what they were.
And it is for Jessica and Rachel and Michael, who I hope never themselves live what the eyes on these pages have had to know.

Most of the names in this book have been changed. They weren't changed to protect the innocent, for, as Kurt Vonnegut points out, the innocent don't need that kind of protection from us. The changes were made to protect those who have already paid enough for what they may have done (they still have to live in Cummins), and to avoid lawsuits promulgated by those who might object to what others have to say about them. No convict quoted in this book asked me to disguise his identity, but it has been necessary to do just that.

Contents

Acknowledgments

Most of all, I want to thank the Cummins inmates and staff, who let me intrude on their crowded lives and asked only that the range of photographs I published show the place as it really is, them as they really are. I tried. Strangers will judge the value of all this, but they will judge how well I have kept the promise.

I want to thank Arkansas Prison Commissioner T. D. Hutto, Cummins superintendent Art Lockhart, and assistant superintendent Mike Hawke. I had the luxury—usually denied (for no good reason) to working journalists and scholars studying public institutions—of being allowed to visit the prison on a number of occasions over a period of four years. I was permitted to photograph and interview freely. Guards were not allowed to monitor my research or interfere with me in any way. Hutto made only one request of me, the same one made by the inmates: that I try to report fairly what I saw and heard and learned.

I also want to thank the organizations that contributed financial support to my studies in the Arkansas penitentiary: the John Simon Guggenheim Memorial Foundation, the American Philosophical Society, the American Council of Learned Societies, the Polaroid Corporation, the Research Foundation of the State University of New York, and the Institutional Funds Committee of the State University of New York at Buffalo. The *Pine Bluff Commercial* and the *Arkansas Gazette* graciously gave permission to quote material from copyrighted articles.

Several friends and colleagues contributed advice at critical points in the preparation of this book, most notably Howard S. Becker, David Dortort, Walker Evans, Michael Lesy, Anne and Milton Rogovin, Lynn Wade, and Kathy Wells. Most important of all was the continuing support from and criticism by my colleague Diane Christian.

Those who contributed most to this book are indicated in the first part of the dedication. I hope only that the work fulfills the expectations they had for it.

BRUCE JACKSON

Buffalo, New York

KILLING TIME

LIFE IN THE
ARKANSAS PENITENTIARY

Introduction

Grady is the second town you reach if you drive south out of Pine Bluff along U.S. 65. Grady has one blinking yellow traffic light suspended over the two-lane highway at its only street intersection. The town consists of two gas stations, a few stores and houses, a cotton gin, and a post office.

Each day a car from the state prison farm comes to the Grady post office. A guard in a blue uniform picks up the mail for the convicts and for the guards and their families who live on the prison grounds. He leaves in exchange smaller bundles of outgoing mail.

Most days, you can spot a gaily bedecked sheriff's Ford lurking in a driveway in Grady or along the side of the road by the railroad tracks near the blinking yellow light. The car has a lot of antennas, sirens, and flashing lights. People talk about it for miles around. It is quite spectacular for so small a town. Residents will tell you that the sheriff will stick it to anybody zooming through Grady: white or black, local or out of state. "It takes a lot of speeding tickets to pay for all that equipment," the man pumping gas tells a visitor who comments on the glistening machine across the way. Even the white cars with official state seals going to and from the penitentiary slow down around that blinker.

The white cars carry prison staff, prison documents, prison inmates. The drivers are not considered law-enforcement officials, and any tickets they get for speeding are their own responsibility. The only official of the Arkansas penitentiary who is also a law-enforcement official is the commissioner, who was made a major *ex officio* of the Arkansas State Police, but even he slows down for the thousand yards of Grady jurisdiction.

Five miles south a sign on the right says you are now in a town named Varner. There is no town named Varner, Arkansas; there is just a sign saying that. There is no building near the sign, no blinking yellow light over the highway, no lurking sheriff. Perhaps there was once such a town or maybe a large plantation owned by a family with that name, but no one there now remembers anything about it.

To your left, directly across U.S. 65 from the Varner sign, is the narrow paved road that goes into Cummins prison farm. The prison property comes right up to the highway and there are several signs advising against stopping for hitchhikers in the area.

Some drivers passing by on U.S. 65 slow down in the hope that they will see something interesting. They rarely do, unless the convicts happen to be working the rice or cotton sections near the road. On those days, the drivers see small groups of fifteen or twenty men in white uniforms working in close rows; near each group is a man in a blue uniform. The man in the blue uniform rides a horse.

Most days the drivers see nothing, for Cummins farm is very large and the men are usually working far from the roadway on the side of the prison near the Arkansas River levee. Most days the only workers in the area are trusties in khaki driving tractors, and they look like farmers working any other large cotton or rice farm.

Some of the cars on U.S. 65 speed up when they pass the prison signs. One wonders why: not even desperate men can leap across a road into a car going 60 or 65, and the utility of going up to 75 or so seems minimal. Perhaps the drivers are merely embarrassed about the place and don't want to look at it, and so decide to get away as quickly as possible.

Most drivers pay the place no mind at all. The cars and pickups maintain their speed and the drivers don't look away from the two-lane blacktop. That is because they are so used to seeing the prison they no longer see it at all: it is to them no different from the farms before and after, they have seen it a thousand times and they will see it a thou-

sand times more. They don't bother to look because they know there really is nothing to see. Not from U.S. 65.

Far across the rows of cotton and beans and rice, you can sometimes see the shape of the distant buildings of Cummins. The distance is deceptive because the land is so flat and the buildings are larger than they seem from the road. From the highway, there is never any motion to be seen at the Cummins buildings.

It is five miles along the curving penitentiary access road before you reach the first of the high concrete guard towers. It is too far for the merely curious to cruise in for a look. No one without serious business there comes as far as the first of the barbed-wire fences.

The fences enclose a large area with many buildings. There are a laundry, a gymnasium, a small cinder-block building with an iron roof that once held the solitary confinement cells but is now a group of workshops. Near the back fence is a small house where some trusties live.

The main complex houses 1,400 adult male convicts. It has two colonies: the West Building, or Minimum Security Unit, recently completed and reached through the central corridor of the main building, and the East Building, or Maximum Security Unit, finished about seven years ago, about fifty yards across a concrete walkway from the east end of the long hallway that cuts through the entire dormitory area of the main building.

It is necessary to pass through five locks to reach the central corridor from the front of the prison. A button in front of the guard in the tower facing the prison opens the solenoid lock controlling the gate through the twelve-foot-high Cyclone fence. The fence is topped with a triple row of barbed wire. (The fence looks easy to climb, but it's not. One can't even approach it without drawing attention, for it is bracketed by an underground motion-detection system that circles the entire compound. If anyone approaches the fence without using the required path in front or the sally-port gate road in back, indicator lights in the tower tell the guard exactly where the movement is occurring.) Once through the fence, one walks across an open yard to the building entrance. In a small room protected by bulletproof glass, a guard controls two heavy steel doors, each with bulletproof windows. He controls the doors' solenoid locks with an array of buttons on a panel before him. The two doors are never opened at the same time, so if someone coming or going gets this far without cause to go farther, his progress can be safely stopped. The two doors and the small space separating them form a very tight cell. The large sections of glass make it appear airy and loose, but it is really quite secure. Past the second iron door is the administrative area of the prison: to the left are the warden's offices and the staff commissary, to the right are the records section and the doors leading to the offices used by parole officers and counselors.

There is another iron door here. It is controlled by a convict with a large anachronistic key. Past him is a long hallway, narrow and poorly lighted. To the left is the auditorium, which on weekends is used as a visiting room; to the right are the offices of the prison photographer, the chaplain, the field major, and the building major. This is the first stop for new inmates: free-world law-enforcement personnel leave their guns at the front picket and escort the new inmates to this hall. The police take off the traveling handcuffs, get a receipt, and go away. The new inmates are stripped, fingerprinted, and photographed. Then they are given a little lecture by the building major. He tells them the convicts are convicts, the guards guards, and any convicts who fail to understand the difference between the two roles are heading for a sorry stay. Inmates arriving at Cummins for the first time receive a slightly different lecture from the one given to inmates who have been there before. The inmates are given receipts for their personal effects, then are sent off to be shorn and outfitted in prison uniforms. They have to go into the main corridor for that.

That requires a short walk the rest of the way down the narrow hall. There is another iron door at the end, this one the first of the traditional heavy prison bars. It too is operated by a convict trusty.

The main hallway stretches a short city block to the right and left. There is a high desk against the wall in the middle; a lieutenant usually sits there and takes care of various things. Near his desk is the entrance to the large inmate dining hall. There are a few other rooms. But most of the hall is taken up by the entrances to the eight large dormitory rooms—called barracks here—perpendicular to the corridor. Each holds anywhere from 85 to 150 men, depending on how many double-decker bunks are currently in use.

Lately the courts have issued edicts saying the barracks are far too crowded, which is true, so the prison authorities have acquired several dozen large house trailers to be used as temporary minimum security units. The problem is, the courts have also been rapidly increasing their incarceration rate, so almost as soon as new housing space is built, the pressure in the old barracks once again begins to climb.

At the front of each barracks, to the side of the large barred walls fronting the corridor, are the toilets and showers; at the backs are the clothing issue rooms and the commissaries. At either end of each barracks, mounted high on the wall of bars, is a color television set. Except for special events—such as the Superbowl—the television sets are tuned to different channels.

The Max (if you are talking with convicts) or the East Building (if you are talking with guards or staff) has three wings. All of them run off a central control area dominated by a large room splendidly arrayed with warning lights, solenoid controls, and microphones and speakers. Guards in this room control the front door, the hallway doors, the doors from the hallways to the wings. They can monitor various kinds of activity in the wings.

Two of the wings in Max are for administrative segregation: protection cases (pretty young boys, snitches who got caught at it, and so on), violent types, aggressive homosexuals, escape risks. The third wing is punitive segregation and is used for inmates serving internal sentences for a variety of rule infractions: insulting an officer, fighting, refusing to work, possessing contraband, and so on.

Most of the cells in Max are one-man, but hardly any have only one man in them. In cells without extra built-in bunks, the less powerful residents sleep on mattresses on the floor. In the punitive wing, all mattresses are taken out each morning, so the inmates have to sit on an iron bunk or the concrete floor during the day; in the administrative segregation sections, the mattresses are left in place. A few of the rooms are fitted with four bunks; most of these have several additional mats on the floor.

Before the Minimum unit was completed, the administrative segregation cells were the best living quarters in the prison. They don't offer the mobility of the large barracks or the constant access to television after work hours, but they have some measure of privacy and some degree of quiet. Both are absent in the main-building barracks, which are all horribly noisy: toilets flush, showers run, people talk and walk and play games, radios and tape recorders and the two television sets and the television sets in the barracks directly across the hall blare away. And there are constant noises from the corridor, ranging from shouts by the turnkey that a certain inmate is wanted at the yard desk to the clanging of the large iron gates.

Minimum is best of all: each inmate is in a private room and there are no bars. One can close the door at night for quiet and privacy, and there are windows from which one may see something of the outside world. The windows are small—too small for even a child to squeeze through—and the outside view is broken by the Cyclone fence and guard pickets, but there is none of that constant human density of the barracks and little of the tight control on movement of Max. The rooms are arranged in circles around centrally located guards who can scan the whole unit, but none of the individual rooms directly faces another.

Even though the prison is densely populated, almost a behavioral sink, it is nonetheless a terribly lonely place. Perhaps the density forces a cherishing of personal space unknown to those of us in the outside world, the free world. Men are careful not to intrude on one another, and only the Minimum unit has a physical structure that legitimizes privacy.

When I first visited the prison in August 1971, the inmates went to the fields in large trucks, jammed in the back like livestock. They stood up in tight mobs for the jolting ride out to the work areas. Now they ride in carts with benches; the carts are linked together and are towed by tractors. The great advantage of the tractor, from the inmates' point of view, is that it doesn't go very fast. When I last visited in October 1975, the field force was clearing timber and brush from an area on the other side of the levee that protects the farm from Arkansas River floods. The carts left the building at 7 A.M. and didn't reach the work area until about 8 A.M.; they started back to the building for lunch at 11 and left again at 1 P.M. They returned to the building at 5 P.M. The work in the intervening hours was miserable, but there weren't nearly so many hours of forced labor as in previous years.

There are no rest breaks. The men get a quick trip to the water cart about once every hour. The guards get water from a water boy who brings cups to them where they sit atop their horses; the inmates later walk to the water cart and drink from paper cups. In 1971, everyone drank from a metal cup; there was one metal cup for the guards and another for the convicts.

If a convict wants to urinate, he shouts, "Pourin' it out here, boss." If he wants to roll and light a cigarette, he shouts, "Lighin' one up here, boss." If the officer agrees, he silently nods, and for a moment the convict stops his work and urinates or lights his cigarette, then quickly catches up with his squad.

The guards sit on horses all day and shout and look down at the convicts, who listen to the shouting and look up at the guards on their horses. They are all out there all day long, except for mealtime: guards, horses, convicts, dogs.

Most of the work is agricultural, as it is in all the other southern penitentiaries: cotton, soybeans, rice, cattle, hogs. The prison has its own school district now and a lot of the men spend half of each day in class. There is a unit that teaches some people how to handle data processing equipment. The print shop was recently outfitted with a lot of modern equipment. The atmosphere in the shops is pleasant and relaxed, but you rarely forget that you're in a penitentiary.

One day on my last trip, when the line was going into the building for lunch, someone wandered too close to a window in the East Building. I couldn't tell if he just wandered off the path or if he were trying to talk to someone inside. The guard outside the fence with the shotgun jacked a shell into the chamber. I heard the *chu-chunk* a good fifty yards away, and I am sure every convict in the yard heard it too. There is no sound quite like a shell being jacked into a shotgun chamber. Almost everyone froze. The man out of position moved back into line with the other workers, but the rider fired the round into the air anyway. "Thereby," a staff member said to me later, "throwing away the entire psychological advantage he'd gotten when he'd jacked that round. There was no need for it: he was just proving he could do it if he wanted to."

There must be a curious pressure on men who every day ride out under the sun and sit and look down on other men, all of them knowing all the while that the only thing maintaining the equilibrium is the gun carried by the man on horseback. Some must wonder what they would do without the gun, and some must wonder if they would actually use it well if the time came when they had to point it at someone and pull the trigger. That heavy constant weight must be a continuing reminder that they are always at the border of a critical test they might very well fail.

Like most of the inmates, most of the guards didn't set out to wind up here. There is not much industrial employment in central Arkansas, and the mechanization of the farms has obliterated the one likely employment option for the younger men in the area. Some have finished high school, some even have a little college, but there isn't much to do with the training. Only a very few consciously entered the field of corrections, intending to make a career of it. For most, it's just a job. They have a lot of role models for the farming jobs they couldn't find, but the only role models they have for the mounted prison guard come from movies like *Cool Hand Luke*. The assistant warden sometimes tells them that prison life isn't really like the movies, but I'm not at all sure they believe him.

There are black guards now in the Arkansas prison. One of them runs off at the mouth as much as any of the so-called rednecks he rides with, which gets some of the black convicts mad. They forget that he has had no one else to learn from, and they forget that the distance between guard and convict is greater than the distance between black and white. One's friendship lines in an interracial group are often confused and ambiguous, but in the world defined by men with guns and men without guns, there is no ambiguity at all. The difference is absolute.

When I started this book, I planned a group of photographs about the people who inhabited one southern penitentiary. It was to be about the inmates: how they lived, how they looked to and for an outsider. I say *for* because any portrait photograph depends as much on the way someone decided to be photographed as on the way a photographer decided to take a picture. Unless one hides behind a long lens or plays sneaky games, it's always a cooperative venture.

I noticed on my contact sheets many images of guards and officials. There weren't nearly so many as there were images of inmates, but then there aren't nearly so many guards and officials as there are inmates. I learned from those images that the guards lived in the penitentiary too, that their faces were part of the record.

I remember particularly one older guard whose picture I

took by the sally-port gate in 1972. He seemed in that photograph mean and harsh. The next year, I was looking around the hog-lot office and he was sitting at a desk talking with one of the convicts who worked out there; they seemed to like each other well enough and the guard didn't seem harsh at all. He told me he had been a farmer for many years but things had gotten too tight to hack it on a small farm, so he'd taken a job as prison guard some years earlier. He was there the day they dug up the bodies for the television cameras during Tom Murton's administration.

One day in 1975, when I was videotaping the garden squad, I saw a white prison pickup truck barreling toward us along the turn row, a tan plume of dust rising rapidly behind it on the bone-dry road. I swung the video camera to the truck, then zoomed in on the cab, and I saw the old guard steering with one hand and holding something in the other. He got a little closer and I realized that what he was holding was an extremely ugly medium-sized snake. It had fangs.

The truck stopped and I yelled, "Don't come near me with that goddamned thing!"

"I ain't comin' near you. I'm just *showin'* it to you."

Most of the guards didn't know what I was doing or why I was doing it or who I might be doing it for. They knew only that word had been passed down from the commissioner and superintendent to let me go where I wanted whenever I wanted, to talk to anyone I wanted to, and they were to stay out of my way. Most did. The last time I was down, a number of guards did wander around where I was working, but I soon realized that they weren't trying to interfere or even snoop, but only to get their pictures taken too. They were right to present themselves, for they are as much a part of that world as the convicts, a part an outsider like me sometimes forgets.

Overt interference was rare, and that usually came from lower-level nervousness rather than administrative interference. Once a construction supervisor saw me walking across a field and told the inmates in his work crew, "Don't any of you talk to that man."

That night in the barracks, several of the men in the crew told me they'd been told not to talk to me.

"About what?" I asked.

"He didn't say."

"Doesn't he know I can just as easily talk to you in the building?"

"He don't know nothing."

I think the main times my presence interfered with normal goings-on came at disciplinary hearings. According to every inmate I talked with, the hearings were milder (more acquittals) and more courteous ("sir" instead of "motherfucker") when I sat in. There was nothing I could do to check out that charge, short of bugging the disciplinary hearing room, which tempted me more than a little but which temptation I rejected because this is primarily a visual book and the visual configurations were the same whatever niceness was added to the words.

Once a lieutenant made a guard put on his tie when he

saw I was about to start photographing. I photographed the man putting on his tie and the lieutenant went on his way.

At one new construction site, the free-world supervisor made a row about my cameras. He said he didn't want me taking pictures except from a distance or in profile—there were to be no pictures in which anyone could be identified. I didn't tell him that profile pictures are fairly recognizable most of the time. He said he wasn't going to have anyone going around taking pictures of *his* inmates. He was obviously demonstrating to those around that he wasn't subject to the same rules as the guards. He didn't know who I was or what I was doing and he assumed I came from some central office somewhere. He didn't care *what* central office: the prison, the state construction fund, the press, the VFW. He asserted his benevolent paternalism against all of them: these were *his* convicts.

"I never take anyone's picture who doesn't want his picture taken," I told him.

"I don't care what you do, around here you—"

He stopped talking for a moment and we wandered off for a few paces. Four convicts on the work crew had been watching the exchange from the partially completed roof of a nearby building. One yelled, "Hey, Bruce! You gonna take our picture or not?" The free-world supervisor tried to make sense of what was going on, failed, and walked away.

Time and again, Cummins prisoners asked me whose story I was going to tell, "theirs or ours"?

"Mine," I said. "That's the only one I know."

Most thought that fair enough, but a few said, "What about the stuff you don't see?"

"I can only photograph what I see," I said.

"What are you going to *say,* then?"

"I'll print the pictures and some quotations from you and them and let the pictures and quotations say what they have to say."

"But which pictures will you print?"

"The ones that say what I saw."

The more times I had that conversation, the more complicated I knew both the questions and the answers were. Seeing is an act, not an event. Like speaking or signing one's name, seeing is something everyone does, but something everyone does differently. It is only when we are in the position of presenting our vision to others that the idiosyncrasy becomes painfully manifest. But it is always there. Ingmar Bergman is fond of quoting Antonioni's line: "Every camera position represents a moral decision."

One photograph in this book illustrates that terrifyingly well. A man stands by some bars; leaning against the bars next to him is a painting he was working on. If you look carefully, you realize he has painted a version of the biblical Flood. The victims are in various postures; dark birds begin to gather in the sky; far off in the distance, bathed in a faint halo of light, is a boat, sailing away. Museums are full of paintings depicting the Deluge. This is the only one I have ever seen that treats the event from the point of view of the victims, those left behind after the only ship sailed away forever.

All but one of these photographs are from Cummins, the Arkansas penitentiary for adult males, located about fifty miles south of Little Rock. The one exception is the young black man in the solitary cell with the redundant chain and padlock on the cage door: that is from Tucker, the Arkansas prison for younger offenders. He was awaiting a disciplinary hearing when the photograph was made and was later transferred to Cummins because the disciplinary board decided his behavior was annoying. It seemed reasonable to let the photograph come along.

About a dozen years ago, some bodies were dug up in a field a mile from the prison barracks. The digging was well attended. Someone there told me that NBC and CBS were on hand when the work started, and the superintendent—Tom Murton—ordered the digging held up until the tardy camera crew representing ABC arrived. The dig was in part bogus—everyone at Cummins knew there were bodies in that corner of the field, for the area had long ago been a graveyard for pauper convicts. (A physical anthropologist from the Civil Aeromedical Institute of the Federal Aeronautics Administration studied the three skeletons and said they had all been buried for fifty to seventy years.) Murton staged the dig to show what sort of operation his recent predecessors had run.

Even though he probably lacked legitimate bones, Murton found a reasonable metaphor for what the place had been like in earlier years: a lot of men died young in Cummins and many of the records that said "heart attack" or "shot while trying to escape" or "escaped, never caught" were lies. The bones unearthed for the television camera may not have been the bones of the men murdered in Cummins, but men were murdered there and one set of dry bones serves as well as another to make that point.

My statements about the Arkansas prison in this book are mostly in the images. But a great deal has been written about the place in the past decade or so, and most of that writing is grim stuff.

Tom Murton, who was for a short while superintendent at Tucker and for an even shorter while superintendent at Cummins, wrote a book called *Accomplices to the Crime,* which accused appointed and elected state officials—charged with management of the Arkansas prisons and treatment of those Arkansas citizens who became prisoners—of behavior easily as criminal or negligent as anything most of the inmates had done. Murton was fired, but the Arkansas Penitentiary Study Commission, appointed by former governor Winthrop Rockefeller, substantiated many of his charges.

In 1969 Federal Judge J. Smith Henley took the previously unheard-of step of declaring the entire prison unconstitutional. That case, now known as *Holt* v. *Sarver I,* again came before Henley in 1970, and in *Holt* v. *Sarver II* the judge expanded his original declaration.

Henley noted the incredible power of convicts over convicts: there were few free-world employees in the prison system and the guns were carried by trusties. When state troopers came to the prison, they had to hand over their weapons to armed convicts, many of them serving time for murder. Inmates received no pay for their work and the only legitimate source of earned income within the prison was one's blood, which could be sold. There was a heavy traffic in contraband and illicit services. Trusties controlled the food, so inmates with money ate well; inmates without money did not. "An enterprising trusty who makes the most of his opportunities can do quite well for himself," Henley wrote. "Some do so well they do not want to leave the institution. While it can hardly be said that the trusty system in Arkansas is a 'free' enterprise system, it is certainly a capitalistic system with some of the worst features commonly attributed to 'Mafia' techniques in organized crime" (*Holt* v. *Sarver,* 309 F. Supp. 362 [1970]). Commitment to the penitentiary, wrote Henley, "amounts to a banishment from civilized society to a dark and evil world completely alien to the free world, a world that is administered by criminals under unwritten rules and customs completely foreign to free world culture. . . . Such confinement is inherently dangerous. A convict, however cooperative and inoffensive he may be, has no assurance whatever that he will not be killed, seriously injured, or sexually abused. Under the present system the State cannot protect him. Apart from physical danger, confinement in the Penitentiary involves living under degrading and disgusting conditions."

Henley had written in the first decision (*Holt* v. *Sarver,* 300 F. Supp. 825 [1969]) that the state of Arkansas had "failed to discharge a constitutional duty" when it failed to take steps to ensure that inmates might "fall asleep at night without fear of having their throats cut before morning." In the 1970 decision keeping the federal court's control over the prison, he pointed to the socially destructive work of the prison: "Living as he must under conditions that have been described, with no legitimate rewards or incentives, in fear and apprehension, in degrading surroundings, and with no help from the State, an Arkansas convict will hardly be able to reform himself, and his experience in the Penitentiary is apt to do nothing but instill in him a deep or deeper hatred for and alienation from the society that put him there. And the failure of the State to help him become a good citizen will be compounded by the ever-present willingness of his fellow inmates to train him to be a worse criminal."

His decision was revolutionary: he said that prison officials were responsible for what happened to the people in their care: "Let there be no mistake in the matter; the obligation of the Respondents to eliminate existing unconstitutionalities does not depend upon what the Legislature may do, or upon what the Governor may do, or, indeed, upon what the Respondents may actually be able to accomplish. If Arkansas is going to operate a Penitentiary System, it is going to have to be a system that is countenanced by the Constitution of the United States" (*Holt* v. *Sarver,* 309 F. Supp. 362 [1970]).

In 1974 the prison administration under T. D. Hutto, who had been appointed commissioner in the spring of 1971, asked Henley to lift the court's injunction. The judge found sufficient improvements in living conditions, inmate treatment, and staffing to lift his order, but the U.S. Court of Appeals insisted that the court's control over the penitentiary continue for a while longer. The Court of Appeals decision took note of the "significant progress and improvements . . . at both the Cummins and Tucker institutions since *Holt II,*" but it said that "there exists a continuing failure by the correctional authorities to provide a constitutional and, in some respects, even a humane environment within their institutions. . . . We find major constitutional deficiencies particularly at Cummins in housing, lack of medical care, infliction of physical and mental brutality and torture upon individual prisoners, racial discrimination, abuses of solitary confinement, continuing use of trusty guards, abuse of mail regulations, arbitrary work classification, arbitrary disciplinary procedures, inadequate distribution of food and clothing, and total lack of rehabilitative programs. We are therefore convinced that present prison conditions, now almost five years after *Holt I,* require the retention of federal jurisdiction and granting of further relief" (*Finney et al.* v. *Hutto,* U.S. Court of Appeals, Eighth Circuit, October 10, 1974).

The court recognized that there had been great improvements under the Hutto administration, but it demanded more: the fact that things were far better than they had been didn't satisfy the requirement that they become as safe and fair as the court said they must be. The new buildings put up in response to the criticism of overcrowding in the earlier decision were not acceptable as an answer to that earlier decision. The reason was that Arkansas courts had so much increased their commitments that the additional inmate population more than offset the increase in room and bed space.

One of the dreadful ironies here is that the prison commitments increased specifically because the prison became so much less horrible than it had been: as soon as judges around the state thought the prisons were no longer torture chambers, they became willing to sentence to prison terms men and women they would earlier have placed on probation. The Women's Unit at Cummins was an even more shameful facility than the main prison: it was one wooden building on a one-acre site in the middle of the giant farm. The building held about seventy women. When plans for the new women's prison at Pine Bluff were published in papers around the state, the rate of female prison commitments increased so rapidly that a new wing had to be designed for the new women's prison even before it was completed just to take care of the increase in inmates. Judges who wouldn't send nonviolent offenders to prison because they detested the old wooden building with its single dormitory room, it tiny mess hall, its hot sewing room, were more than willing to *double* their commitment rate when they felt they were sending the women to the nice clean well-lighted place being built at Pine Bluff. The same thing happened in the men's prison when drawings of the new Minimum appeared.

The problem is similar to what happens when highways in and out of large cities are significantly widened: the problems worsen, they never improve. The wider highways make possible more bedroom communities farther out, so more people leave the city and drive in each day to work;

the new highways almost immediately are as choked as the old ones were, and the cities die even more quickly as their limited resources try to handle increasingly complex population problems.

When I first visited Cummins in July 1971, there had been some major changes from the days that produced Judge Henley's documents. Most of the brutality was gone. (Not all: inmate "building tenders" still did some of the guard's dirty work, as they do in most American prisons now that courts around the country have told wardens they cannot permit their staff to torture convicts. But even in New York's Attica prison, which in 1971 was a far more brutal institution than Cummins was, overt brutality by guards has been severely diminished.) The food was decent (far better than when Murton first came, when inmates never saw meat or milk). The work seemed tolerable, though dreary and uninstructive. But the buildings were, as now, crowded, and most of the men carrying rifles in the fields were convicts.

I've visited the place six times in the past four years and there have been many more changes. No convicts hold guns over other convicts, new buildings have gone up, the house trailers have for a while eased the pressure in the barracks, there are more recreational and educational programs, beatings are rare and often result in immediate dismissal of the guards involved.

But the mere fact that the commissioner's office says inmates should be treated fairly doesn't mean that on the line—in the fields and in the barracks—people will be treated fairly. It would be nice if bureaucratic orders worked like that, but they don't. Less than two years ago, a young boy died in Cummins because he was sorely maltreated: he was sent to the fields after being shifted from Tucker for punitive reasons, he had little sleep and little food, inmates harassed him with the tacit approval of the field guards. "That boy died," one member of the prison board said later, "because nobody out there really cared enough. How do you make people care?"

Cummins is still a prison, and *nothing* changes that. The improvements make the place bearable, never decent. Nothing makes prisons decent, at least none of the prisons I've visited, and I've visited a lot of them. In all that crowded and moiling space, life is terribly lonely. Even in the very best of prisons, whatever and wherever they may be, time is hard. The poverty of life in those poisoned years does unnamable things to the spirit, and so far none of those fine court decisions has touched that aspect of prison life at all, not in Arkansas, not in Virginia, not in New York, not anywhere.

But—and this is something some outsiders find hard to keep in mind—prison is a place where people live, where they go through the various acts of life most people out here go through. They make friends and enemies, they find ways to avoid suffocating boredom, ways to feel significant; sometimes they laugh.

People make nests, try to personalize the impersonal. No one, for example, is allowed to tape or tack anything to the walls in Cummins, but decoration goes on nevertheless. In the barracks, many locker boxes are decorated with pictures and drawings inside and out. Sometimes the inside pictures are of family, sometimes they are nude images from *Playboy* and *Penthouse* and *Escapade,* sometimes they are both. (Walker Evans said, "I would have taken photographs of all of the locker boxes, all of them. You could do a whole book on just those locker boxes.") In the Max, administrative segregation cells sometimes have long strings of such pictures suspended from wall electrical and ventilation outlets—the top picture is jammed under the cover plate and the others are taped to one another. The administration takes the position that inmates can get anything that is allowed to go through the mails, so the erotica is sometimes complex and surprising.

People manufacture things. Someone had a steamboat he'd made for his son; a tuft of cotton glued to a cardboard tube served as smoke. Another man made houses from little stones he picked up while working in the garden. Another made picture frames from pinecone sections. The Polaroid Corporation sent me several cases of SX-70 film packs and I spent a few days making photographs for people to send home. Someone asked me one day for the empty packs; the next day I found them serving as frames. The economy is very lean and men make do with depressingly little.

There are even pets. One day in 7 Barracks I saw someone I knew as Dago walking down between the bunks holding a long string. Attached to the string was a small rabbit. "Dago, what are you doing?" I asked.

"I'm walking my fucking rabbit. What do you think I'm doing?"

Someone in the laundry had cats; someone in one of the shops had a pair of desacked skunks.

A prison community is no less a community than any other. The main difference between this and most other communities is that here mobility is not volitional. It isn't volitional in the military or in some clerical orders either. In prison, mobility is dependent on outside agents: parole boards, psychologists, some stranger's class-action suit filed a thousand miles away.

I think it would be easy to photograph any prison and show it as a hellish place. Probably one could photograph *any* complex institution and show it as hellish. There is some truth there, but also something of a lie, for such a representation would hide a basic fact of life: even in hell, most people spend their time getting by, not wallowing in agony, and most of the residents are people, not caricatures in turgid TV dramas. I've tried to show some of that in these photographs.

I would like to think that the photographs are objective, but I worry about objectivity in enterprises more analytic than parking a car or weighing buckets of mud or long division. A photographer, however much he seeks to document something real, spends a great deal of time learning and deciding what he will and won't shoot, what negatives he will and won't print, what prints he will and won't show others, what juxtapositions of images he will permit on a gallery wall or on published pages. The great deceptive ability of photography rests in the apparent verisimilitude of the photographic image. Sure, it really happened just like that, those people were in those configurations at those times. But there were other times, other configurations, and you don't see them unless I want you to.

My friend Howard S. Becker insists it is impossible to do serious social documentation with a camera without some informing theory: there are too many chances for selection, options for inclusion or exclusion, too many choices made.

My theory would probably begin with my belief that prison doesn't do anyone much good. There are some people who have to be locked up; they are just so nasty we can't afford to have them running loose. That's too bad, but that's the way it is. I think it is reasonable to keep such people off the streets until they learn some other way to get by. The problem is, they don't seem to constitute a very large portion of the people behind bars. I keep thinking that a society as rich and sophisticated as this should have some other way to deal with people whose systems are poisoned by heroin or alcohol, or with people who are too dumb or uncharming to make it well in the competitive world of stores and offices and schools.

Most people in prison are damaged by the experience in ways the Chi-square analyses of social scientists can't begin to calculate. For one thing, the qualities of behavior needed to make it well in prison are exactly the opposite of those needed to make it well in the free world—initiative, curiosity, independence—and that is why rehabilitative programs are always irrelevant or peripheral, why they fail.

Some people in prison learn to read and write and they are therefore better equipped to deal with our world than they were before, but since it costs about $12,000 a year to keep someone locked up and the total cost of tuition and room and board at places like Harvard and Yale and Penn now runs about $7,000 a year, that seems a stupid economy if mere retooling is the goal.

I think the primary function of prison is to hurt people, and prison succeeds at that quite well. I doubt if most people who run prison think hurting people is their job; most of the administrators I know try to make prisons as humane and helpful as they can. The reason they fail is that there is no way to make a cage humane and helpful. So they keep on trying and they keep on failing and they always look a little puzzled when they find that not only do the inmates hate them, but so do the free-world people whose social garbage they are charged with secreting. I won't say anything about the guards and wardens around the country who are deliberately mean and cruel: they've been written about by others who know them better than I, and I suspect they're in a minority anyway. I worry more about the decent people in "corrections" who manage to do evil things because of fear: fear of the convicts, fear of their fellow workers, fear of the press, fear of the legislature, fear of their own sure knowledge of how easily they might be wearing that other uniform.

The problem is, there is no way to do the job decently, because the idea isn't decent. The best one can hope for is a parody of civility, a parody of society.

And that is another part of the theory behind these images: as I said before, people *live* in prison. They don't live well, but live they do. They make spaces for themselves, decorate what they can, define as private the tiny areas they can manage to control; they negotiate hustles and seductions and friendships. For most of the outside world, the inmates are locked away for a period of years and are totally invisible. Except for Attica in 1971—when for a little while angry inmates spoke directly into the living-room television sets before they were murdered—there have been no live broadcasts from these places. The information on television, in the press, and even in books like this is packaged and arranged neatly by people comfortably outside and far away from those high walls and barbed-wire fences.

For most inmates, one day follows another, and each day is filled with the things days everywhere are filled with: work, sleep, filling the body up and emptying it out, keeping alive and staying sane, making as few compromises as possible, and hoping tomorrow's compromises will go down easier than today's

My theory would end with this: Some of them look like you. And me.

I. THE IMAGES

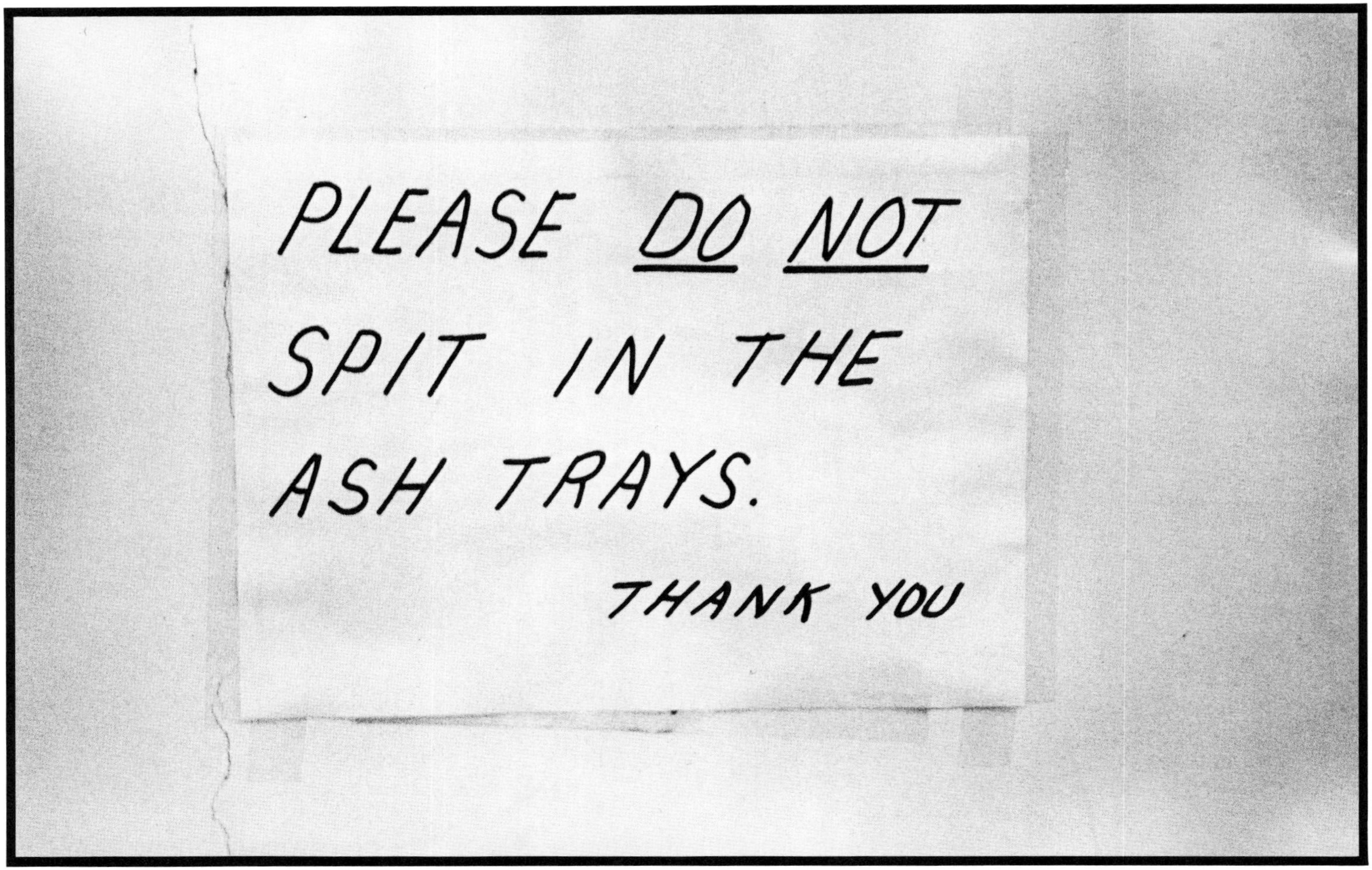
PLEASE DO NOT
SPIT IN THE
ASH TRAYS.
THANK YOU

ATTENTION
This is your bath room keep it
Clean all towels and articles of.
    clothing.
Will be turned in to the picket.
Not left on the bath room floor.

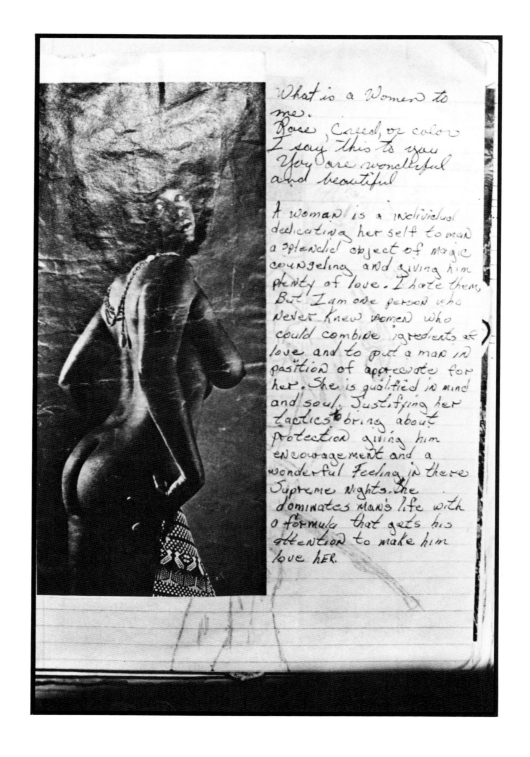

What is a Women to me.
Race, Creed, or color
I say this to you
You are wonderful
and beautiful

A woman is a individual
dedicating her self to man
a splendid object of magic
counseling and giving him
plenty of love. I hate them,
But I am one person who
Never knew women who
could combine ingredients of
love and to put a man in
position of appreciate for
her. She is qualified in mind
and soul, Justifying her
tactics to bring about
protection giving him
encouragement and a
wonderful feeling in there
Supreme nights. She
dominates man's life with
a formula that gets his
attention to make him
love hER.

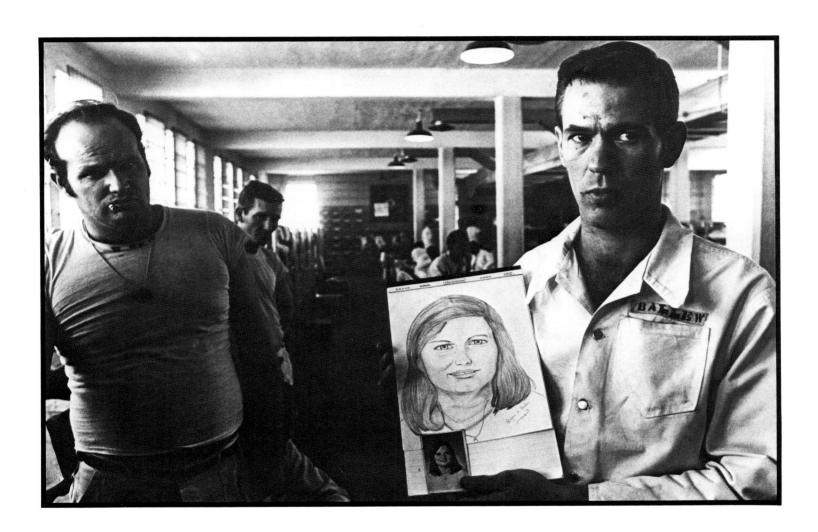

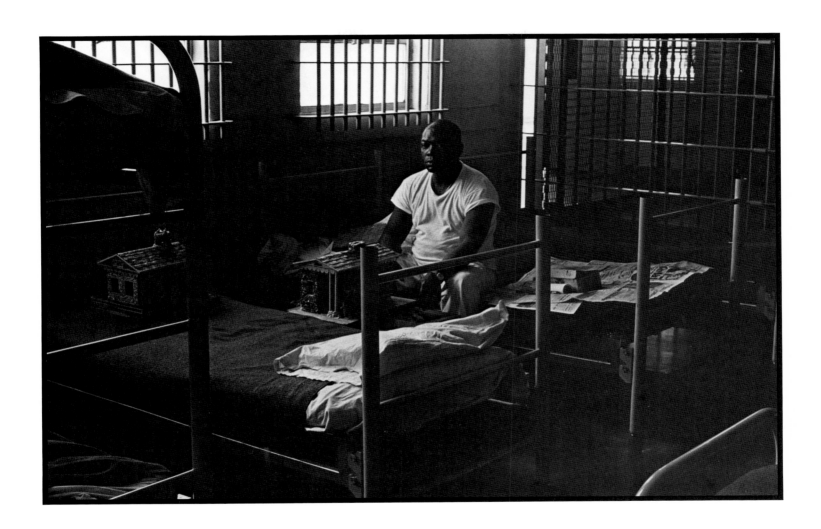

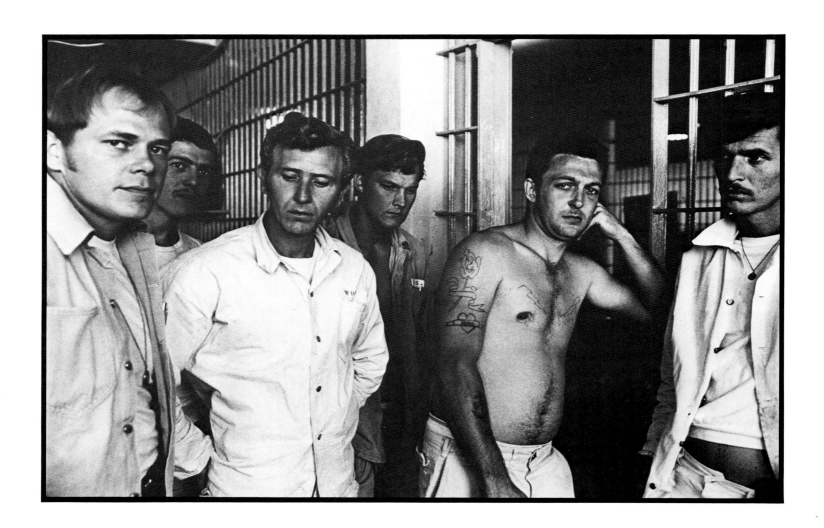

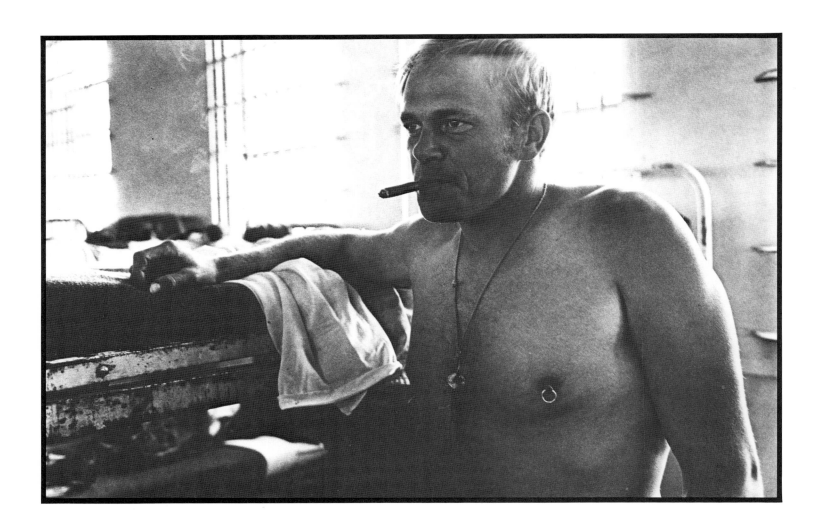

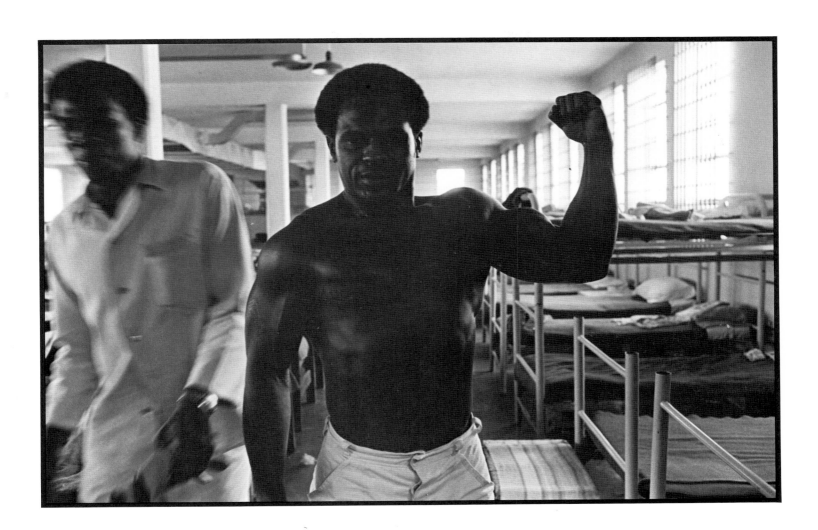

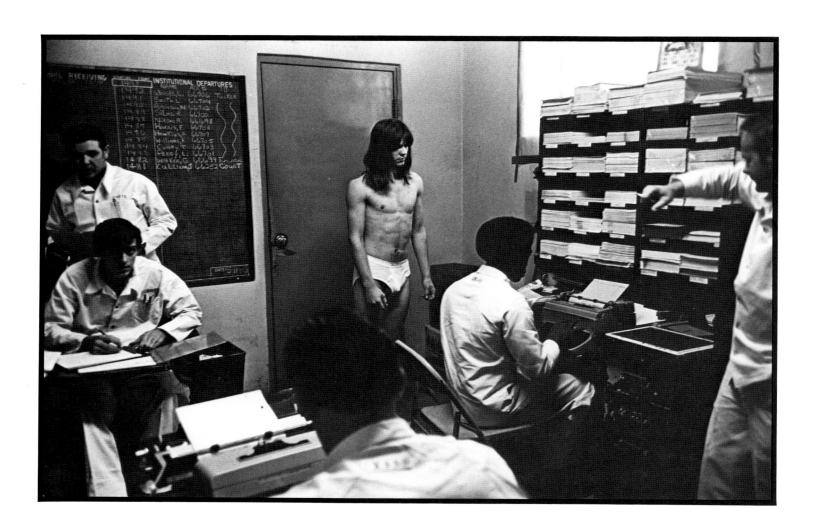

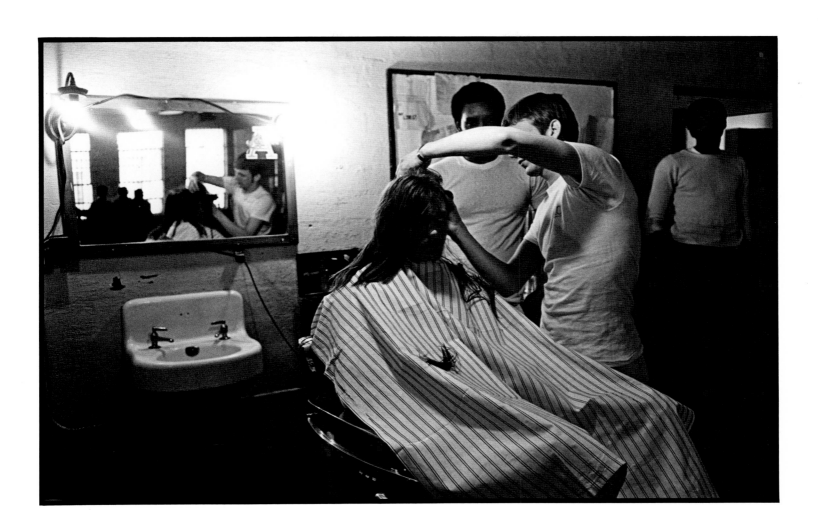

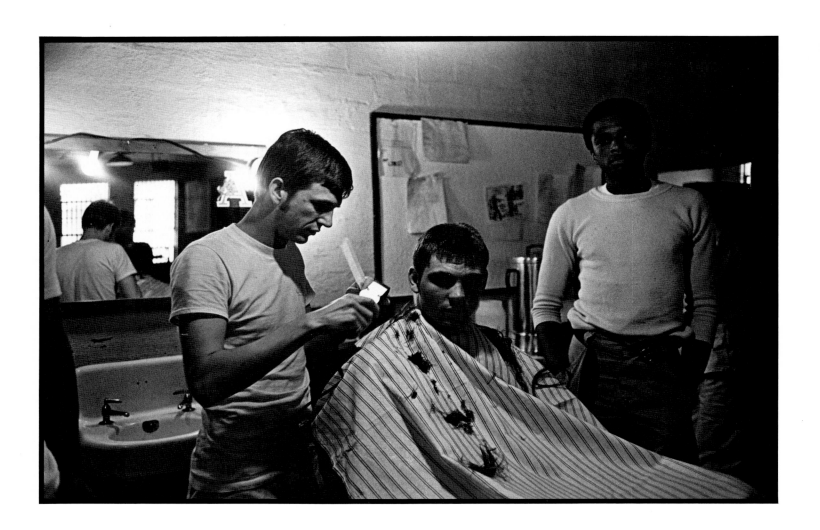

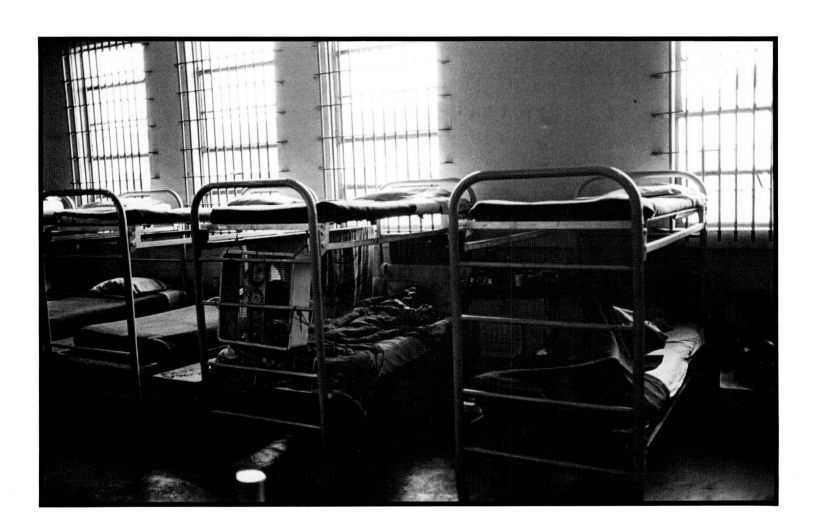

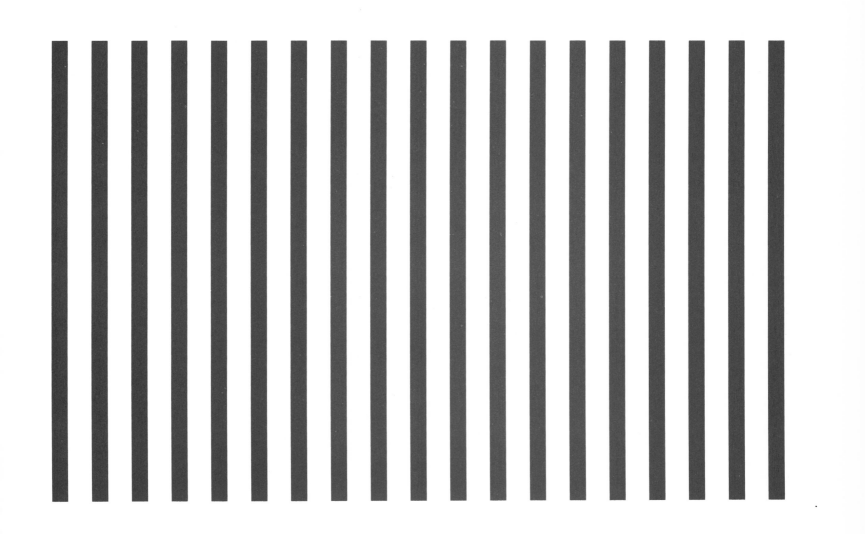

116

130

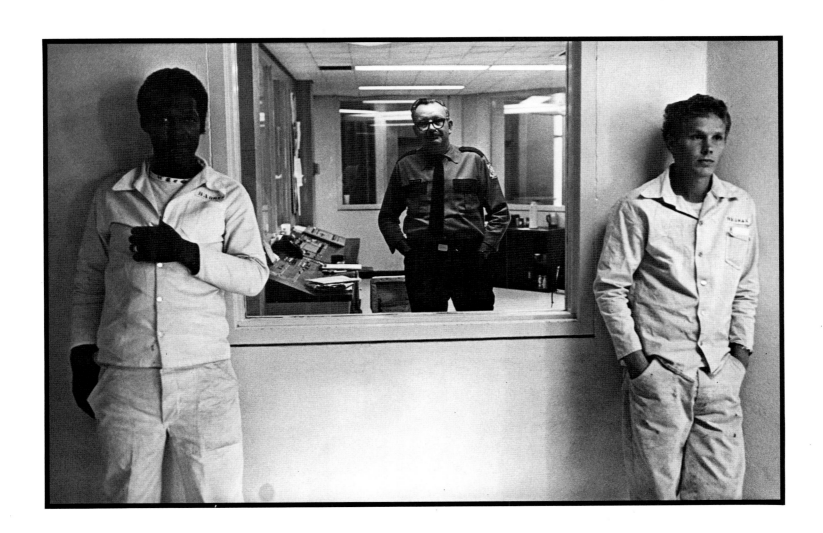

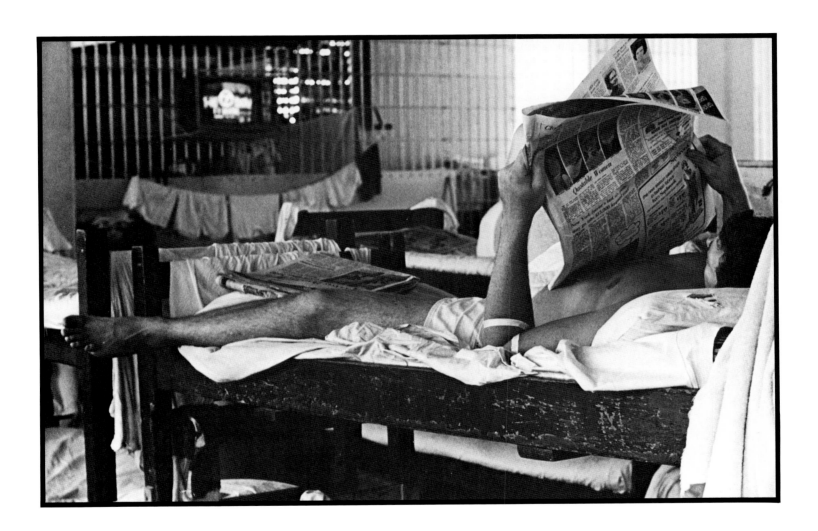

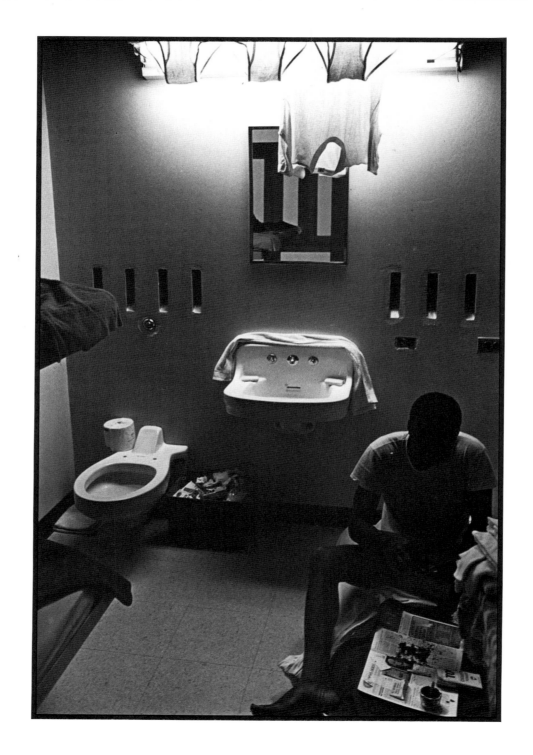

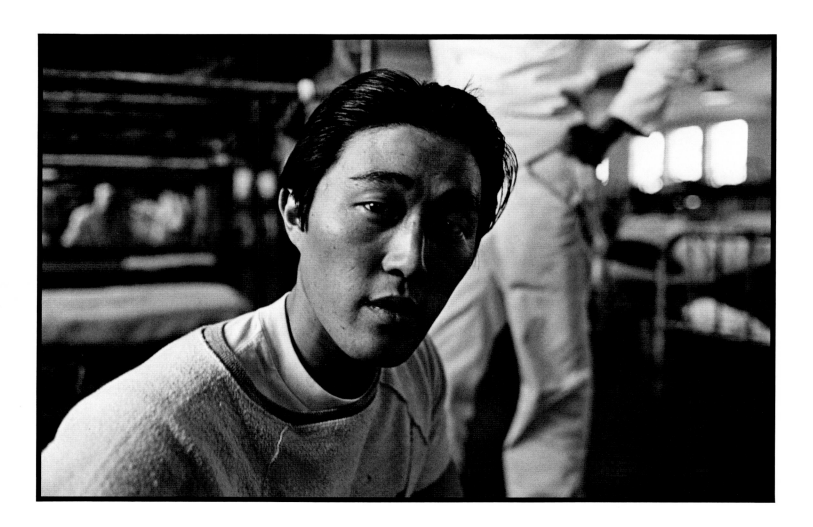

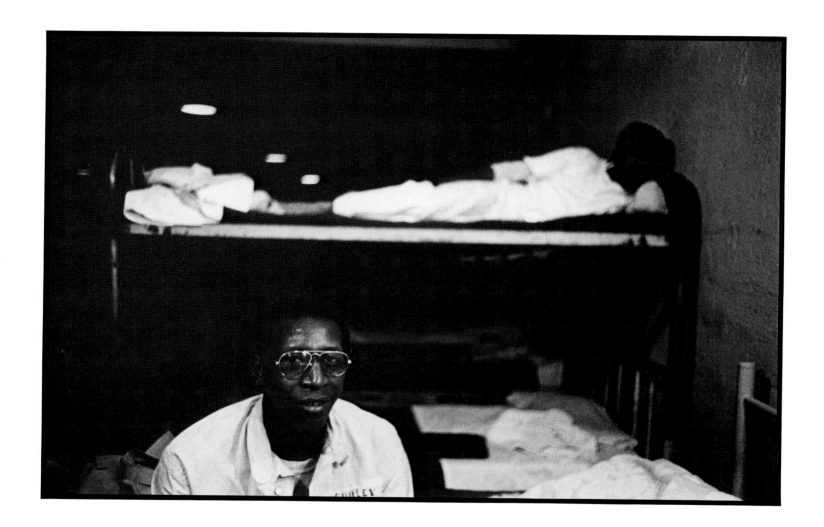

II. THE VOICES

My understanding of Cummins prison comes not only from what I saw there but from conversations with inmates and guards and from local newspaper articles, documents in prison reports and files, and the various court decisions relating to the many problems at the institution over the past decade.

The images in the book make their own statement, but the copies of documents and transcriptions of conversations that follow help give one a sense of the historical and contextual backgrounds. Most of the items are self-explanatory; I have supplied introductory notes for the few that seemed to need such notes.

Cummins and Tucker were always brutal places. Violence and physical deprivation continued well into the 1960s. The statements on these pages document the range of past horror and present problems. The words are of racial and sexual violence, of grim styles of human management that lasted so long for only one reason: no one outside with power cared enough to change things. There was only one reason for permitting violent convicts to run the prisons all those years: it was the cheapest way to run the place, and money was more important than human life.

Arkansas was not alone in that vicious economy, but it happens to have one of the few American correctional systems that has been willing to let outsiders come in to document what happened in the past and what is happening now. As I read through these pages, I wonder again and again what terrible secrets would be found behind the walls of Attica or San Quentin or Joliet. The styles of horror may vary with the regions, but I really doubt that the fact or intensity varies at all.

Some of the problems named in these documents are gone. Some others will go as the prison hires and trains more qualified staff, and as more buildings are constructed, more school programs inaugurated, more farm machinery purchased. But even so, the basic problem of running and inhabiting a prison will remain: some men are controlled by other men with keys and guns, and all of them live in dense communities few of them like. There will always be fights, escapes, self-mutilations, rational and irrational explosions by staff and inmates, hatred.

That is because one can never strike out at the real source of the pain, the one ineluctable fact of prison life—the absence of freedom—and all the attacks therefore are directed at the wrong object. The most pitiful thing about prison violence is that it almost never accomplishes anything, because it is almost never directed at an object that has any real power.

More than anything else, I think these statements display the enervating impotence that poisons the lives of guards and convicts and administrators alike.

1. Cooter's Yellow Pad

One day in 1973, a man waved to me from the small truck-scale shack opposite the cold storage locker on the road that goes from the main prison building through the Freeline (the small cluster of houses for guards and administrators who live with their families on the prison grounds) and all the way out to the cotton gin and levee at the back border of the prison property. I drove up the ramp and found it was a man called Cooter, who had been turnkey in the main hallway the last time I had been down.

We talked awhile and then he said something odd: "Look, you got to understand this: I didn't think you'd ever be back here no more."

"OK. But why do I have to understand that?"

"Because after you left last time I got to thinking about those questions you were asking me about what it was like here in the old days, and after I got this job I started writing some of them things down."

"How come?"

"I don't really know. I didn't think I'd ever see you again, so it wasn't for you. But I didn't want to forget those things neither, and I'm alone out here most of the day and there's not much of anything to do when the trucks aren't up being weighed. I think about a lot of things out here."

"May I see what you wrote?"

"You can have it. Now that I done it, I don't need it no more."

He handed me a legal-sized yellow pad. There was close writing on twenty-seven pages.

"Can I quote some of this in my book?"

"You can do anything you want with it. I'm done with it. But you got to keep in mind I didn't think I'd see you again. I didn't write it for you. I wrote it for me. What I wrote in there, them things happened like that."

This is what Cooter wrote:

Monday October 21st 1957
the day that I entered the Ark. State Pen.
no. 4906 term of three years
Crime—Strong Arm Robbery
from Lincoln County, Star City, Arkansas

The sheriff of Lincoln County and Capt. Lockman—better known as "Pappy" because he was in his middle sixtys but he had retired or quit, I don't know just which—they took me over to Cummins which is in Lincoln County and the sheriff is just a little kin to me. Mr. Tom Walker was the sheriff's name and his brother was the superintendent of the prison until he died in the fifties. But he could still do you some good. Capt. Wayne Henry steped up to Capt. Tom's boots when he died.

So when we got to the prison Mr. Tom ask me if I was ready to face the music. I was so scared I could hardly talk, but I said, "Yes sir." It sure was a sad looking place. Every building was white and you could see guards everywhere you looked and I was doing plenty of that. Mr. Tom and Pappy Lockman took me in the front and turned me over to the convicts that was in charge of the fingerprinting and the mugging. They took my picture and then fingerprinted me and took what little money I had, which was about five or six dollars. I don't know what happened to it, but I do know that I didn't get it back. I had a carton of cigarettes which they let me keep.

When the front office was through with me a trusty told me to follow him. So here we go down a narrow hallway. We went about a hundred feet then we came to a bigger hall. This was the hall between the barracks. There was 1-2-3-4 barracks. There was a few trusties out in the hall and there was a big desk on the left side of the hall. We stopped there. There was a trusty sitting at this desk. His clothes was starched and ironed and his boots looked like they had a spit shine on them. He took my name and said, "Put him in 4 barracks and put him on punk row." When we got down at the barracks doors I had to take off all of my clothes. Then the door was unlocked and I stepped in and I got my shorts and undershirt, socks, belt and a pair of air force flight boots back and the carton of cigarettes, then the convict who was leading me around took out his pocket knife and cut the notch out of my boot heel. [Southern convicts traditionally wear shoes with notched heels so trackers can tell which footprints belong to an escaped convict and which belong to everyone else.] It must have been about 10:30 by that time.

After I got a bunk and the barber got through with me we went to dinner. It is a good thing that I wasn't very hungry because all we had was soybeans and cow peas and some greens of some kind. I ate a few of these things which had no seasoning at all. There was just water to drink. We went to the barracks and I took a nap. At 3:30

we went to supper. The chow was the same as the dinner was, except when we came out of the messhall I had to take my boots off and my socks off, then I had to take everything out of my pockets and then be shook down by a trusty. When he got done with me I went down to the barracks. The convict that was in charge of the barracks told me to catch my bunk because the longline would be in in about an hour or so. It was just about 6 o'clock when they started coming in.

Each man counted when he came in the barracks door. If there was 10 men in the barracks the first man said 11-12-13 and so on up until every man was in the barracks that lived there and then the door was locked. There was a gun room about 25 foot below the door in the end of the hall. When the count was all cleared and they was sure nobody had ran off, then the guards all came in and put their shotguns and rifles into the gun room.

Then in about thirty minutes I heard someone up in front of 1 barracks hollering for dear life and it sounded like a shotgun was being fired. I heard one of the men behind me say, "Poor bastard, that's Big Abe slanging the hide." Big Abe was the longline captain and he was a big brute of a man over six feet tall and well over three hundred pounds. That man had no feelings at all for a convict. Then he got through up in 1 barracks and came down to 4 barracks and got three out on the hall floor and began to whip one of them. They had to lay down on their stomach and the hide was supposed to hit you on the buttocks, but Big Abe was catching him from the top of his head to the bottom of his feet. There was more begging out there in that hall than in any church I have ever heard. These men were bleeding when they took a bath.

The reason that they got the beating was because they didn't pick enough cotton for the day. That was not all that got the hide.

I heard then the other convicts talking about three that had to be took to the hospital. One of them had been shot by one of the convict guards. That didn't say if he lived or died.

A few days later there was me and seventeen others transferred to Tucker. That is a smaller prison up in Jefferson county about 40 miles from Cummins. And a tough S.O.B. I found out in just a matter of hours. When we got over at Tucker it was dinnertime. They run us in the mess-hall if it could be called that. We set down to some more cow peas and turnip greens which was just about half done. But one of the cons said, "There is meat in the peas," so I got the bowl and found the meat all right. It was worms, but there was plenty of them and we ate them.

There was this little fellow that came over with us. He was a real small kid. But he was 27 years old and about 4 foot 11 inches tall and weighed about 96 pounds. He was as tough as a boot. He said he had just got out of Jefferson City, the Missouri state prison. That little fellow said he hadn't had a smoke in two days, so I gave him one. He thanked me and said, "I will wash your laundry for you if you will get me a pack of tobacco." I told him I would to-night. I had sold my flight boots over at Cummins before I left. I got three dollars for them and I was getting broke.

That evening Capt. Bobby Brinkley loaded us up and took us to the Warren field where the longline was picking cotton. When we stopped we jumped out like a bunch of hogs. There was guns everywhere I looked. The guards was very young, maybe 23 or 24 years old. You could see their ribs. They was underweight. I knew if the guards was in this shape they sure wasn't feeling worth a ——.

Capt. Brinkley ask me if I could pick him any cotton. I told him I could. He said it is a damn good thing I could. I was just about the biggest in the transfer. I was six-one, I weighed 160 pounds at that time, but I lost down to 136 in 2 months. That evening the short hairs—that is what they called all of us—just helped the others on their rows. I weighed up 65 pounds that evening, but I caught the hide the next day. That was the worst ordeal I have ever had in my life. I got 12 licks from Capt. Brinkley because I couldn't keep up. I wasn't the only one out on the turn row, just about all of the short hairs was out there. We was going our best. But Capt. Brinkley said that was not good enough. There was grown men crying and cursing. They had just about give up.

Then Captain Floyd Billings drove down to see how things was going. Captain Brinkley left and it was better after that because the riders took one of the girl-boys over in the cotton trailer for a little romping.

In the next week the cotton was all picked. We had some corn to pull at the county line which was five miles from the building. We got to the corn field early that morning. It had rained that night. There was water in the middle and we had to tie a knot in the sacks to keep from getting the corn wet.

I filled my sack and gave it to the man up in the trailer. He poured out the corn and layed it on top of the side boards and it fell off next to the guard line. When I went to get it the shotgun guard fired at me and one of the .00 buckshot caught me in the arch of my left foot.

I fell to my knees. This pillhead helped me up and out in the field. By that time it was getting some feeling back in it. My foot was so big in about an hour it looked twice its size. Capt. Brinkley started to whip me for getting shot. He told the rider to build him a damn fire so he could cut that shot out of my foot. When the fire was burning he got out his knife and stuck it in the fire. The truck driver told him if he cut my foot he was going to have a lot more cutting to do when he was finished with me. Capt. Brinkley changed his mind and made me walk to his truck which was about 300 yds. away and put the guard in the cab with him and me in the back. When we got to the hospital I had to walk in and the convict doctor asked what had happened. Capt. Brinkley said that "The sorry S.O.B. got over the guard line." Which was not true. But there was not much I could say or do. Brinkley did get to cut my foot open. I believe that was the worst sound and feeling I have ever seen or heard. They didn't even have anything to kill the pain. I finally got loose and Capt. Brinkley said, "I hope that it rots off."

I stayed in the hospital for about a month. When I had been there a month or so I got a visit from my mother and father. But there was a guard with me and I couldn't tell them what was wrong. That pellet stayed in my foot. When I got able to go back to work, Capt. Brinkley carried us over in the Judy hole. He said we was going to scrape up some cotton. We was supposed to have been through picking. It was on a Saturday. It was in January and cold as hell.

Capt. Floyd had gave orders to let the longline catch all the rabbits that we could since all the work was just about done.

I was picking in a row next to a Indian boy. He was maybe 26. He was a good convict. His name was Frank Neal. Frank was from Oklahoma. One of the riders, J. L. Montgomery [a convict guard], was on a horse after a rabbit. I saw J.L. coming and I told Frank to look out but it was too late. J.L. had run him down. I saw that he was in pretty bad shape. Blood was running out of his ear and the skin was broken in three places. I helped Frank up but he was just about half knocked out.

Capt. Fisher was helping Capt. Brinkley with the line that Saturday. We got Frank to Capt. Fisher's truck and he stayed there the rest of the day. That night Frank said Capt. Fisher had told him if he wouldn't say anything about what happened to Capt. Floyd, he would see that he would get turned out as trusty. Frank asked me what I thought about it so I told Frank they are trying to cover up something. So Frank kept his mouth shut and in May of 1958 Frank got turned out on a highpower over the plow squad. I had got turned out do-pop [a half trusty] and was working at the horse barn. There was some long hours but not too much work.

Then one day about 12:30 o'clock a horse was running

down the road behind the horse barn over across the bayou. It looked like old Smokey, J. L. Montgomery's horse. J.L. was the rider over the plow squad. Frank was the guard and there seems like there was another guard by the name of Ross with Frank.

I had heard a shot from a rifle but that was nothing to get upset about. I caught Smokey and there was a shirt on the saddle. Then in a few minutes I saw the plow squad coming in but there was just one trusty with about maybe eighteen men and that was Frank riding old Olphant Boy, the same horse J.L. had run over him in the Judy hole. Frank put his men on the yard and turned his .30-30 into a tower guard and went back to trusty barracks and lay down on his bunk and told Wiley Tolson, "I just killed a sorry S.O.B. and I am glad of it."

We went from the horse barn over to the yard and got the mules and brought them to the barn and unharnessed them and put them in the pasture. In just about 45 min. a deputy sheriff out of Pine Bluff, Ark., Jefferson County, came over there and made an investigation and Cap. Fisher went over at Two Camp where this happened and got J.L.'s body in the back of his pickup. He stopped at the horse barn and said, "Cooter, take that pair of mules and wagon over at Two Camp bridge and cover up the blood that J.L. lost."

So I got a shave and got over there and run the dogs off and covered it up. Then I went back to the barn and got the shirt that was on old Smokey. It was J.L.'s shirt and in the shirt pocket was a letter to Capt. Floyd. I opened the letter after about a week to see what was in it. The letter started out

Capt. Floyd.
I would like very much to talk to you because my life is in danger. If not mine some one else's life is. Me and Frank just can't make it here on this plow squad. There is bad blood between us if you will talk to me.

Thank you
J.L.

I just put the letter back in the shirt pocket and put the shirt inbetween the double walls of the saddle room since it was too late to do any good for J.L. Later on I went back to talk to Frank after he had been charged with first degree murder.

Frank said he just couldn't get over that sorry S.O.B. running that horse over him. I asked Frank just what happened. He said that everybody was eating and the rank men was sitting down in a line or in two lines facing one another and he Frank had old Olphant Boy standing behind him but he had strayed off about twenty feet and when he went to get him he took a hame string and was slapping him across the nose with it and J.L. had told him to leave the horse alone. And that is what started the trouble. Frank said that "J.L. got his old .44 that he had tied to the saddle on old Smokey and I pulled the hammer back on my .30-30 and took aim on him. The men was between us. I shot one time and the bullet hit right in the

175

middle of the men but it didn't hit any of them. They all layed down. And J.L. run and got under Two Camp bridge. Then he asked me if he would lay his pistol on top of the bridge would I not kill him. I told him that I wouldn't. So he put the gun up on the bridge where I could see it. I told him to come out and he came out with his hands up over his head. I raised my rifle and let one drive. He fell and I didn't think he was dead so I walked up to him and kicked him to be sure he was. And he was. So then I did what I had to do next. I started my men in and Ross run off and left me. I started to kill that S.O.B. but I knew I was in enough trouble. So I just let him go."

It wasn't too long until Frank went to trial. He was tried in Jefferson County at Pine Bluff. And it looked like everyone in the plow squad was against Frank. There was enough. Frank got the electric chair. I think that Frank was the first man in the history of Arkansas to get the chair for the murder of another convict. If he wasn't I never heard of anyone else. I know that Frank had Capt. Wayne Henry against him. If it had been any other way it would have been life or 21 years. But it wasn't.

There was a lot of heat on one trusty fussing with another. Some of them even got ranked. [demoted from trusty status back to regular inmate status]. Some of them asked to be ranked.

Capt. Floyd turned Russel Short and Tony Jones and two or three other men out. And some smart snitch told Albert Maples that they was going to take the long line and hit them [escape]. So Albert was the yard man and he took the old .45 sub Thompson and slipped down in the Warren field and layed in a thicket all day waiting for them to make the break. But it didn't come. When Tony and Russel found out about Albert laying and watching them they put their guns up and went back to the longline.

Then July finally came around and I got back in the hospital. I was getting some corn out of a crib and I jumped out of the crib with a sackful on my shoulder and I stepped on a corncob with my right foot and I layed my ankle flat on the ground. It took about thirty minutes to get to the hospital. The doc kept me that evening.

While I was there Capt. Brinkley brought a kid into the hospital. It looked like he would go maybe 180 pounds. And he had just come over from Cummins. The kid had got too hot and Capt. Brinkley had beat him until he passed out and he decided to bring him into the hospital and try to get the temperature down. But the doctor or what you might call him told Capt. Brinkley that he couldn't do him any good so Capt. Brinkley and two trusties drug him out to the truck and carried him over to the cold storage which was just across the gravel road. I watched them drag him out of the back of the truck and put him in the cold storage. Then Capt. Brinkley goes on back to the Judy hole to butcher up some more of the short hairs.

About 2 o'clock Dr. Scola from Cummins came over and came in the cell where I was. He said, "Son, what is your trouble?" I told him that I had turned my ankle. He looked at it and said, "That looks pretty bad." And told Sandy the doc to keep me there for a week or two. Then he ask if that was all he had to look at today. Sandy said, "Dr., Capt. Brinkley put one in the cold storage about thirty minutes ago." Dr. Scola said, "God damn him."

He left out of there on the run. His chauffeur got the wagon and went over to the cold storage. They put him in the back and out of there they went. We never seen that kid any more so I don't know just what happened to him. But Capt. Brinkley lost his job over that.

Thing began to get better after that. Capt. Brinkley was as sorry a man as you could find. He even looked sorry. He is so sorry that Hobart Williams has a bullet hole all the way through him. Brinkley was so damn lazy he didn't want to whip the boy. So he got Spike Patton to do it. But Hobart got up and started running and Bob Lee Watson put a .30 caliber bullet in him for no reason at all. But you didn't have to have a reason. Just being down here in this god forgotten hell hole called Arkansas State Prison. You was damn lucky to ever see the free side of life I can damn well tell you that. There was a lot of them that didn't you can count on that.

When I had a year done on that three I got a parole out of Tucker. I left there on Oct. 20th 1958. My mother and daddy came and got me. I think it was on a Monday evening. I wasn't out very long until I run up on one of my girl friends and we was married January 24, 1959. I lived my parole down. But I was right back in that hell hole again. I entered the Cummins unit on February 13th 1960. I just had a year. I think the charge was grand larceny. I copped out for one year anyway.

entered Arkansas State Prison
Cummins February 13, 1960

Another sheriff carried me over this time. It was still run the same way. By the convict. The same convict as last time came up front and got me again. And back down that little narrow hallway to the barracks and we stopped at the yard desk. The yardman was all slicked up. He got my name and told me who he was. And on down to 4 barracks. They told the convict that was in charge of 4 barracks to put me on Punk Row. So I was just a little smarter than I was the first trip so I spoke up and I said, "I am a punk mobber. If you don't go for what I say just stick around a while and you can damn sure find out." But I was laying it on just for the fun of it. I never did get in that bad a shape. Although I seen plenty of it go on and there was no "rape" in it.

On February 14, 1960 the yard man had me and some of the other short hairs up in 1 barracks cleaning it up a little. And a buddy of mine was brought back. He couldn't seem to keep his business straight on parole. Billy McCoy seen me in one barracks and he give the yard man something to let him in there with me. But I wasn't assigned to that barracks and didn't want to be. That was a hot barracks. There was more heat on men in there than there was on John Dillinger. But I got assigned up there and Billy McCoy too.

But I didn't stay but eight days before I was transferred back over at Tucker. I knew that I was going to Tucker. Just a few days before I was to go to court I and my wife paid Capt. Floyd Billings a visit. I told Capt. Floyd what was up and he said, "Cooter if you get any time you have your wife to call me just as soon as you get the time and tell me. And I will call and have them send you over just as soon as you get there." So she called him. And he told her that he would get me over there and he did. I believe it was on the 20th of February that I got over at Tucker. It was 2 o'clock in the morning when we got over there. We got a little sleep but not too much.

I was still a little shook up because this time I had a wife. And I was just a little worried about her. She was just 15 years old. But I knew that she was a good kid. But good people get messed up some times. But there was not much use in me worrying about that because there wasn't anything that I could do. I had asked her to try and stay with me. She promised that she would. And as far as I can say or could see she did. I guess every man that goes to any prison will ask his wife or girl if she can stay, 'and I just believe that every woman or girl friend will say yes. But I am sure that she did just what she told me she would do.

Capt. Floyd was off of the farm the Saturday that I got there. So the long line was working on the yard cleaning out some ditches for just something to do. So we was out of the building when on a Sunday night Capt. Floyd came over and called me up to the bars and talked to me for a while, then told Albert Maples the yard man to give me a jumper and overhalls and assign me back to the horse barn. So at 4 o'clock in the morning the night floorwalker woke us up and out to the barn we went. I knew all the

things there was to do because I had worked out there about 9 months before. We had a different rider. This one was a bitch on wheels if I ever saw one. J. C. Sherman. He was about 5-1 in. tall, about 115 pounds and had a nose about 4 in. or it looked that long and would rat his momma off. I finally got him a little scared of me and we had no trouble.

Then one day Capt. Floyd sent for me to come up to his office. He said he had the D.A. on the phone and he wanted to know if I would take a year to run c.c. [concurrently] with the year that I was doing. If I did he could settle it right there so I told him that I would. That was the outcome of a little trip that one of my old buddys and me took. Got drunk and borrowed some money without asking anybody. It was a motel at Conway, Arkansas. Capt. Floyd called my sister and asked her if she would tell my wife and daddy if they would come up and get me and take me to Conway for the sentence. So they was there the next morning. And I went to Conway and got another year. The three months that I had already did was dead time. They say a man can't do dead time. Well in Arkansas you can do as much as the courts want you to do.

When I got back at Tucker Capt. Floyd put me back at the barn for three days. Then I was carried to Cummins on the second Sunday in May 1960 for a new number. I can't remember that one. But it was up in the 5000s. I had to stay overnight because I missed my ride with the Commissary truck that was going back to Tucker. That was because the yard man didn't understand the deal. Capt. Floyd called over and raised a little hell about it so they put me in a car going to Fort Smith and I got to Tucker on Monday evening.

Capt. Floyd told me he had a new job for me if I thought I could handle it. He said he would talk to me about it in a few days. On a Sunday night Capt. Floyd asked me if I could handle a .30-30 rifle. I told him I was one of the best. And I thought I was. And still do. So I was put out with the plow squad. There was another guard by the name of Bill Clay. And I was back with the rider I was under the first time I worked at the horse barn. His name was Frank Ramsey. Frank was doing a life sentence for rape. But he was a fair guy. We had a good understanding between us. We had some good boys in the plow squad. But the water-boy had a little heat on him. He had tried to escape once while he was in the tractor squad. So he had been busted from do-pop to a rank man. They moved him off of the water cart and put him to plowing.

Any time they got out of their lines they had to get a wave from one of the guards or the rider. J.T. didn't do that. He got out and started toward a ditch and I yelled at him but he kept on going so I busted a cap. The bullet struck him in the leg, his left leg just above his knee. I knocked him down. The rider came up and asked what happened so we told him. Capt. T. R. Forest took him to the hospital and Capt. Floyd came over and ask what had happened so I told him. I told him I didn't have any more shells. I told him that I couldn't fire a warning shot because I just had the one shell. So Capt. Floyd went to the building and got me twenty rounds.

In about a week J.T. was out of the hospital and Capt. Floyd came down to the no. 2 well where I was guarding the plow squad and asked me if I would sign a accident report on the shooting so it wouldn't hurt the man when he went up for parole. I signed the report and when J.T. went up for parole he made it and got out. Everything looked like it was going to be smooth for a while.

Then along the first of July or the last of June we had put the plow squad on the yard for lunch. I was sitting beside the west tower trying to eat lunch and some of the longline had come in and the line guards was up above me in a shooter shack. It was John Crocker and Bob Dalton and Roscoe Marley. I heard a shot but couldn't tell just where it came from. So in a minute or two the yard man Stanley Green came running out of the building with a pistol. Then I knew something had went wrong so I dropped my tray down and run out in the road. Then Bob Dalton came out and Roscoe Marley came out but John Crocker didn't come out so then I had a damn good idea what had happened.

We all knew that John and Bob had been having trouble over a crap game in the barracks but I didn't think it was enough for anyone to get killed over. Roscoe said Bob stuck the end of the barrel up under John's chin and pulled the trigger. It was a sawed off 12 gauge shotgun and was loaded with 00 buckshot. It took the whole front of John's face off and a part of the top of his head.

When Capt. Fisher came over and got him they throwed him in the back of the truck like a damn dead dog. They put Bob back in the death cell for a while. When they took Bob to trial in Pine Bluff, Jefferson County, he was convicted and got a brand new 21 years. It might not have been so bad but John had already made parole and was just waiting for his release date to come around. It hadn't been but about a month since John's wife and little daughter had come to see him. John was from Texas. His wife was good looking and they had a pretty little girl. I think John's body was sent to a funeral home in Pine Bluff and John's wife came and claimed it.

Boy, the heat was on then. If a trusty was caught fussing with another trusty you could bet they wasn't a trusty any more. Then for about two weeks the shotgun guards had to carry their guns with the breech open. That way there couldn't be a accident. But that didn't last too long. The shooting started up again.

But I got off the plow squad and went to work as the night sheriff. It was a good job. I worked at night. I had to check the picket guards and feed them. There was two tower guards and the hospital guard and there was one down at the front gate. I checked them regular. They was some good men. A little young, but you could depend on them. I got just about anything that I wanted to eat on this job. And I was out by myself. I stayed on this job until I left the prison.

One Monday morning in October of '60 I was coming in from the main gate and was at the back door of the mess-hall where the east tower is. I had given my .38 to the guard and was going over to see what was wrong with the guard in the west tower. I couldn't raise him. Stanley Green was supposed to be working that tower. He had been up all day on a Sunday because the trusties carried the rank men over for their visits when we went to work that Sunday night. I told Green and Tom Golding that I couldn't tell them to sleep but I wasn't going to check them until 2 o'clock. So I went over and got in the laundry and went to sleep. I woke up at 1:30 and got up and went by the hospital and woke Tom up and woke Green up over in the tower. He said he could make it now. I went and ate dinner or whatever it was at 2 o'clock in the morning and went down to the front gate. I took a cup of coffee with the gate guard and started back to the kitchen so I could let the barn crew and the dairy crew off. I had a six volt battery light, so I signalled the west tower but he didn't respond to it. So I tried again but still no response so I said to hell with it he has just gone back to sleep. By that time it was getting close to five o'clock. I went up to the east tower and asked Pokie if he could get a answer from Green with the spotlight. He tried but done no good. By this time the barn boys had brought the highpower horses out. I went over to see just what was going on. I pitched a rock up in the tower and couldn't get a answer. So when I turned to go back to the kitchen I put my light over in the horses and I spotted the stock of that damn big .30 cal. rifle. I didn't know what to do except get to hell out of there. And I did just that.

Capt. Floyd was coming across the bayou bridge and he seen me running across the yard and when he parked behind the messhall I was coming out the east tower. Capt. Floyd said what in the hell are you doing. I had a .30-30 carbine then. So I told him that Stanley Green was out of the west tower and had that .30 caliber rifle with him. Capt. Floyd said don't kill him if there is any way around it. Then Capt. Floyd said, "Cooter don't take any chances because Green is doing 10 years and has a holdover for armed robbery in Missouri and I think that carries a life sentence." Boy that shook me up good. It was still dark and nobody was going up on that .30.

By the time daylight had got there Green had left. But he left the rifle leaning up against the tower and that made me feel better. Because I knew that I was going to have to go on the hunt since he was one of my guards.

Grady Smart the dog sergeant came up with the bloodhounds. They wasn't much good to us though. The line rider and a few more trusties went out after him but he was not armed so there wasn't too much to worry about. Herman Wool had already said that if he could find him he was going to blow his goddamn head off. Because Smart wanted to make the parole board. He was to go up on the next board. He had ten ten-year sentences in the beginning but got all of them run into one and had been there quite a spell. So I kind of believed what he said and I knew that Green was not armed and was helpless.

We hunted him from about five o'clock until 11 o'clock that morning. Everybody had give up except me and Herman Wool and Grady Smart. Herman was up in front of me and Grady Smart was out in a field. When I came across a road ditch the little willows lapped together and made it hard to see up the ditch, but I bent over and saw a pair of work shoes. They had a notch cut out of the heel. I knew that I had found Green. He was asleep. I believe if Herman hadn't of made the statement that he had I wouldn't have woke him up. That was the hardest thing I ever did. Because I knew what was going to happen. But I got down

there with him. I got him awake and asked him if he was ready to go. He said he was. I shook him down. But I knew he didn't have anything so I told him to stay close to me. I fired 2 fast shots. That is a escape shot. Herman and Grady came running after him, but they didn't get him. I put him in the back of the pickup and we went to Capt. Floyd's office.

He slapped him around a little but he didn't get the hide. Stanley had told me before we got in that he wasn't trying to get away. He was just trying to get more time so they [Missouri authorities] would drop that hold over on him. So I told him that he had damn sure done the right damn thing to get more time.

The state hadn't tried him when I got out on Dec. 9, 1960. I left on a Saturday morning. It was raining and cold as hell. My wife and my daddy and sister came over and got me. They was a little late so Capt. Floyd ask me if I had any money. I told him that I had 3 or 4 dollars. He said, "If you want to borrow ten you can get it and send it back or bring it to me." Then the office boy said that my wife was coming through the gate. I said that I never would come back to that damn hole.

But things didn't work out that way.

I used to go over to Tucker and visit when I got ready. Capt. Floyd told me that I could get in just any time I want to. In June of 1961 I had a wreck and lost my left arm. The state police had pulled my driver's license and had stuck two or three charges on me. So I had my wife call Capt. Floyd and see if he could come to the hospital. He did. And ask me what he could do to help me. I told him what had happened and he said that they would drop all the charges against me and give me my license back to me. That evening they did just that.

Then all this crap came out on Capt. Floyd about the [Tucker] telephone. I would have to see it happen before I could believe any of it. I know that the hide was there. I seen it and I also got it. But that other crap was being used by the cons I believe. I can just say one thing. I believe

Capt. Floyd was a good man. He treated me like a son. But I never did lie to him. He never did ask me to rat a man off. I guess he knew who to ask and who not to ask. Capt. Floyd must have did a lot of changing from 1962 up until 1967 but I didn't see him after 1962 until I seen him in Little Rock on TV when he was coming out of the courthouse after his trial. Where he got a suspended sentence.

2. It Don't Do No Good To Start a Riot

Lee: "I got my skull fractured. . . ."

I came down here in 1965 under Dan Stevens. I went to Tucker. You had to come here first and I stayed here about two months before I went to Tucker. I was eighteen years of age.

Over here it wasn't too bad. They just used the bullhide over here. You couldn't raise your head up out in the field at all, you had to keep your head down. Because if you raised your head up, you got the bullhide. We had one warden here, he liked to get inmates inside a car, get their head inside the window, then raise it up and beat their heads.

After two months I went to Tucker, which I figured would be better than Cummins because Cummins was pretty hard, you know.

When I got there I went directly to the cotton field. Floyd Billings was out there and he asked me, "How much cotton do you think you can pick?"

I said, "I never have picked any cotton."

He said, "Well, you're fixin' to get a hook of it."

So he put me in two-spot. In two-spot you have to pick eighty pound or more or get your head whupped with a hoe, a hoe that's tapered off kind of like a blackjack. So I picked about forty pounds.

He whupped my head. He first comes out there, he kicks you about four times till he gets you down, kicks you in the head, kicks you in the stomach, and finally gets you down there on the ground. And you can't do nothing 'cause the highpower got a rifle right down on you [the inmate guard points his rifle at the man being beaten] ready to kill you just in case you strike back at the rider. The rider was an inmate too.

They had the inmate do the kicking?

Right. The inmate done all the kicking. There was just three free-world guys over Tucker: the one that was over the field and the superintendent and another one that was over the horse barn, stuff like that, which I never did have the opportunity of going there 'cause I was in the longline.

So he put me in three-spot. Three-spot had to pick fifty pounds. So I picked fifty, fifty-five pounds. Went on up there. And the rider, he had what you call a girl-boy behind me. And he looked at my cotton sack and said, "Twenty pounds." I knew I had fifty-five pounds in there. What he did, it had to come out even in the books for the pounds that was on the trucks, so he gave the pounds to his girl-boy. I got my head whupped again.

They starts at one end of the field and starts goin' all the way across the field whuppin', said, "Well, I'll meet you at there."

We had one inmate, he started hitting 'em with one end of a shovel. Not the wooden part, but the other part. Started hitting 'em in the head and swinging like a wild man.

We had a thing, a picket, which was a line back there and no one was allowed behind it. That's where you got all your whuppin's at. He said, "Where you from?"

I said, "From Pickett, Arkansas."

That automatically reminded him of the picket. He said, "You're on the picket tonight."

So that night I came through the door over at Tucker.

You had to pull all your clothes off out in the hall for shake-down, spread you cheeks, things like that. You had to count coming in, like fourteen, fifteen, and sixteen. And this guy in front of me, he didn't say it loud enough and I misunderstood him, so I said "fifteen" when it should have been "sixteen."

So the floorwalker said "Lee, I want to see you back there in the back for a few minutes." I didn't have no clothes on. I went back there and he went in the bathroom and had a big old stick, a mop stick with tape around it. He took me to my knees the first time. Then he talked to me for a few minutes, told me I missed count, and then started hitting me again and I fell unconscious.

When I came to, I was tied up back there on the bars, just hanging tied, spead-eagled. And he kept me like that all that night and half the next day. Without any clothes on.

The food that we had was mostly rice. They dumped in hot peppers and that thing was the hottest food that you have ever eaten. And sometimes we had this breakfast, dinner, and supper. And there wasn't such things as milk. We never seen a glass of milk while I was there and we never seen any meat while I was there.

How long were you over there?

I went back and forth. When I got my skull fractured—

How'd you get your skull fractured?

By a ax handle, a brand-new ax handle.

In the wintertime, we had an Indian, a full-blooded Apache, and the only way that he could get warm was by hit-

tin' up, warmin' us up. The hoes back in them days was gooseneck hoes. If they break, all you had to do is chop a tree down, which we did, and you stuck it in there, put in a nail and hemmed it, find a piece of glass or something to get all the knots out of it and the bent places, you know.

One day we was chopping grass and he put a horse here and a horse there and the inmates had to come between these two horses and every time we did these riders would whup us on the head.

Just for the hell of it?

Just for the hell of it. To make us up tight, for which they got brownie points from the warden. And I got my skull fractured.

Back then I got whupped five, six, seven, eight times a day, with sticks, ax handles, mop handles. Everybody did—or paid money. It cost three or four hundred dollars to keep the sticks off your head.

When I got my skull fractured—it was a Friday—I left the blood on the side of my head. I didn't take a shower. And my hands was frostbit because it was in the wintertime and we was picking cotton and we didn't have no gloves. There was no such things as gloves here. And hands was just cut up and busted from the frost.

My parents came on Saturday and I showed them the hole in the back of my head which they had to carry me from the fields to the building for. And they went to Governor Faubus and had me transferred back over here.

Did they put you in the hospital?

No. They took X rays of my head and sent me back out to work.

Just about the last part of the time I was over there we was building this kitchen. The old kitchen, you had to watch where you stepped or you stepped down to the ground. It had holes in it. And Floyd Billings, he came at every meal and he had a big chair where he set at and watched everybody.

I had a toothache one day and I got about halfway between buildings and the hospital. Floyd Billings stopped me and said, "Lee."

I said, "Yes, sir?" I'd never talked to him. I didn't know he knowed anything about me because I never had talked to him.

He said, "Lee, you're doing fifteen years for a sex charge."

I said, "Yes, sir."

He said, "What in the hell's wrong with you?"

I said, "I got a toothache."

He said, "You ain't go no durned toothache. Just trying to get out of work."

When I got over there, they hooked me up on a crank-up telephone. They had a table they put you on, and they cranked me up. They hook one wire to your toe and one to your thing and they crank you up. It's just a little hand-crank thing, like an old telephone.

The food that we ate, we ate all our food out in the fields. Dirt and dust and wind—I don't care how windy or raining it was, the water just dripped down in the food or the dust went right in the food. It wasn't nothing but rice or oats, something like that. We had just about the same thing three times a day. And we had gravy but the gravy was so sour. It might have a little milk in it, but it was sour. You couldn't eat it because it was so sour. And the beans was black-eyed peas with the worms curled up there on the top of it. Someone would say, "Well, you're getting some meat for dinner." Sure enough—it was worms that we was getting.

It didn't matter how cold it was. If it was ten below zero, if it wasn't snowing we went out. The reason why we didn't go out when it was snowing is the snow was white and so was our clothes and somebody could escape.

And there wasn't no such thing as writ writing. If somebody wrote a writ, it probably meant death. The first one that I know that wrote a writ was Churchill Summer, who wrote one on the whip, and he went through worlds of hell after he wrote it. But it did go through and this is where the stopping of the hide came in, through him, the writ that he wrote.

Murton, he believed in giving us food. We had good food: chicken, mashed potatoes, things like that. But he gave us a spoon and fork and a knife to eat with, breakfast, dinner, and supper. The knives didn't last but about two weeks. There was more killing during the year he was here than in any year. All the knives disappeared within two weeks 'cause every inmate had a knife.

And from what I hear—I didn't hear Tom Murton say this myself, but I heard from another inmate—Tom Murton said it would be better for an inmate to have a knife to protect himself in the prison. When they had shakedown, I guess there was two hundred, three hundred knives out of one barracks. Even guns was found in the barracks. And the next day, they'd have another shakedown and find that many more.

One reason was, they didn't shake down the trusties.

I was inmate doctor over here the last couple of years I was here. How I became the doctor was, when I got transferred from Tucker back over here because of my skull fracture, they put me in the garden squad for a while, then they transferred me to the old dairy. And in the old dairy I got my hips busted up. What I did, I was on a two-by-four between a pair of mules and I went through a barn door and I didn't get down on the tongue in time and I got caught between the two-by-four and the top of the door. I spent two months in the hospital. The doctor, he kind of liked me and he let me be the inmate doctor.

This doctor, he was from Pine Bluff, and everytime he came he was drunk, we had to put him to bed. He'd give us five or ten dollars every time he came. But he was so drunk we had to put him to bed. And I done all the operations, which I didn't know how to do. I just learned it from another inmate, a trusty. I done all the shots. We kind of went crazy with the shots. We sometimes gave out three or four hundred shots of antibiotic a night—people just lined up because they had a little cold.

When I was in the old dairy we dug up two bodies. That was before I went back to Tucker again.

Tom Murton was over there. Tom was all right in a certain way, but he done something very bad. Letting them have those knives.

The dead bodies, the warden made us fill it back up and dig someplace else. We was out burying a dead horse, but we knew they was human because of the skeletons.

A kitchen job back then cost you two or three hundred dollars. You could pay it five dollars a week to the convicts. This was to stay out of the longline. These wheels like the yard man—we got a free-world man now, but then it was a convict—all he had to do is go to the superintendent and the superintendent will agree with it and he'll put you on a job. But it cost money.

And on the farms it was inmates who had all the guns around here. I remember one time, I never told too many people about it, there was a little fourteen-year-old boy ran off and he hid under a bridge. And the inmate, what you call the longline rider, told him to come out from under the bridge, said he wouldn't shoot. The boy came out from under the bridge, but he shot him full of holes. And, what I hear, they buried him out in the hog lot and said he escaped. That was on Tucker.

Everybody was high then. They was taking dope, shoe polish. Which you can do, I've seen 'em do it, shoot shoe polish. And I've seen 'em shoot Campho-phenique, and I've seen 'em shoot aspirin or anything they can get their hands on. And the inmate people that was working over in the hospital, they was selling it to them. Lay-ins too. [A lay-in is a document from an official or medical officer saying an inmate doesn't have to work in the fields.]

I never did sell any pills, but I did sell lay-ins. It was benefiting to me and benefiting to the inmates that was out there getting their heads whupped.

What would you sell a lay-in for?

Forty, fifty dollars for maybe two weeks. I had the power to put them in the kitchen or vegetable shack.

The superintendent over there at Tucker called me up there one time and he said, "Lee, you're making money back there. I'm up there and making no money at all. I want some of it. I want a cut."

I never did give him a cut, but the way he talked, he wanted a cut.

And we had an assistant warden, he'd come back there every week for hormone shots. To keep his thing up. It takes five or ten minutes to give a hormone shot. It's like syrup, real thick, and you have to give it in the hip.

An inmate that had time, he didn't have to stay here very long. Because inmates ran the record office. They could give you all the time. Come in here and be out the next week. You could buy your way out. Which many and many a one of them did.

I, myself, I lacked twenty days of getting out of Tucker. I went up to the front myself and put twenty days in my own jacket and got out twenty days early. That's what I'm talking about.

They kept me there four years and eight months on a fifteen-year sentence. That's quite a long time, but I guess they needed me after I learned the hospital work.

I have seen maybe fifteen killings myself since 1965.

Most of them that I've seen was stabbing. The first one that I seen was in the barracks down on the white end. They had the colored separated from the whites then. And it was over gambling. We allowed free-world money in here. In one hand of poker you could see five, six hundred dollars. I seen money coming out of this barracks in ten-gallon fruit jars. "Brozine," we called it "brozine" that they used to have.

This man had a knife, I guess about a foot long. And his head was half cut off. I started to pick him up and his whole side was completely cut and my hand went inside to the wrist. He was already dead 'cause every time his muscles moved the heart would just pump the blood out the side.

I had a pair of tennis shoes on, I remember. I started getting dizzy and when I got outside, out in the hall, I passed out. I had never seen a dead man before. I think that was the first one I ever seen actually butchered up. You could take your hands and go right through his arms, you know, where he tried to stop the knife. He ran on up the bars there, he was after two of them. About a month later, the one that done the killing, he got killed himself. He got killed out in the hall. Two inmates came up behind him and stabbed him in the back.

And I seen quite a few killings over at Tucker when I was over there right in front of me. I was watching TV one night when a colored guy came up behind another and stabbed him thirty-some times, and then hit him up against the bars and broke his jaw. He still lived, after that I don't see how. Blood was running out his mouth. I don't see how he lived, but he did. He was a little short truck driver.

I seen a little fourteen-year-old boy get killed over there. This was done by the same inmate that killed the one out in the hall that I told you killed this other man. He killed one over on Tucker because he had a glass eye and the colored boy called him a one-eyed cuss word and he went back there and done him in, stabbed him twice in the heart. I was the inmate doctor then. He was dead before he even got off the floor.

The homosexuals here now, it's not as bad as it was. Then, a boy between the age of thirteen, fourteen, fifteen, sixteen, seventeen, they all became homosexuals. I mean they all was took care of by a older man for sexual acts. I seen two boys, they was brothers, they both got stabbed in the heart. They went up to the warden and said, "This man's trying to fuck me back here."

The warden said, "Well, you shouldn't be here. You shouldn't a got your time if you didn't want nothing done to you."

That's the way the wardens was back in them days.

When Murton was here you worked an hour and you rested maybe five, ten minutes. Now, they don't let you rest at all. You go out at seven-thirty and come in at five o'clock and work all the time you're out there in the fields. I think they should give a person at least a little break out there. I'm in the garden squad and we don't work as hard as the hoe squad does.

The food was much better back in Murton's days. The food is terrible now. You can ask any inmate that. Knives was the only thing hurt Tom Muton.

What about head strumming, did Murton stop that?

Right. But they still had the hole. I spent thirty days in the hole one time. I got in trouble. I done thirty days on bread and water and they had to carry me out because I was so weak. In the six years I've been here that's the only time I've ever got in trouble.

I try to keep my business straight. It don't do no good to start a riot. It don't do no good to fuss with the free-world people out in the hall because what they're here for is to keep you in here, like a jailer. That's their job. No one can help me but my parents and my lawyers and the people out there pushing with me, trying to help me. These people down here, to me, all they're here for is just to keep you in here and you might as well go along with them as long as you're here.

People who go for riots, they don't do no good. They just lose all their good time and get classified class four. They don't get no good jobs and it doesn't do a bit of good.

3. The Sorriest People on Earth

Sam: "They done everything to me but stuck a ham bone in my ass. . . ."

I drove up here first time in 1959, got out in '65. Been back here this time since November.

I'm a diabetic. I can go sometimes two years without having to take that insulin, but then my sugar count will go 'way up on me and I'll have to go on medicine. Well, I went on sick call over there and that's why they got me on that Tucker telephone. I went on sick call because I could tell when that diabetes was hitting me and I went over there to try and get them to put me on medicine.

They put you on one of them hospital tables. About eight or ten convicts get on each side of you and hold your ass down. Back there then, a convict, he's the one that wired your toes up to it. And he's the one that done all the crankin'. He was the convict doctor. He was just a pill roller, not a *real* doctor.

I've gone to work with a hundred and four degrees, damn near died in '64 here. All of us had that yellow jaundice that year. They wouldn't give you nothin' but aspirins. Right now they work you as hard as that old administration as far as work goes. Damned sure do. Just not as many hours.

They done everything to me but stuck a ham bone in my ass and call the hound dogs.

When I went in for the treatment for the diabetes they told me I was a goddamned liar, nobody got sick on this farm.

This old convict doctor had a pet coon down in the hospital and if you said anything insubordinate, he'd set the coon on you. That sonofabitch could tear your ass up. Coon's name was Oscar. I never will forget that mean sonofabitch. You could hit him, knock him all the way across that hospital over there, and he'd come right back at you.

They had a field superintendent here at that time they called "White Gas" because he drove a little ole white Chevrolet. And he'd call you over to the car on the turn row and say, "Stick your head in here a minute, I can't hear you." You stick your head in his goddamned window and he'd roll his glass up on you and whip your head with a blackjack.

Correctional Officer Day: "I know what's in there already: some graves."

There's no comparison, hardly, to when I first came here. They worked out in the field in what they called longlines. Had about two hundred to a group. And it was all controlled by inmates—inmate guards, riders, and one free-world man, one warden, be out with them, that'd be all. And there'd be around two hundred of 'em. Now, there be anywhere from fifteen to twenty in a group, and one man rides a horse and controls them, see. That way.

When I first came here we had lots of escapes and now it's almost a thing of the past. Hardly ever have escapes any more.

I first came here August the first of 1965. Before that I was farming. For nine months I was here I worked as night warden in the building. I was the only free-world man on duty from five in the afternoon till five in the morning. By myself all night, see. Now they have, well, you been up there and seen how much security guard they got now. Back in those days, inmates run the building at night, see, all I had to do is tell one what I wanted done and they'd go on and do it. Guards and all. They had the guns and the keys. Inmates even had keys to the building. Everything. But now it's changed considerably.

I been under seven superintendents since I've been here and I hope to be here a few more years anyway. I'm sixty years old, sixty last November.

How has it changed for you? Before you had inmates as guards, now you have free-world people. How else has it changed?

Well, we have better living conditions. Better for the inmates. We have better food to eat, better clothes to wear, shoes, just better all the way around for them. Now they have a rehabilitative program, which they didn't have before. There's a new school for them. The legislature passed a bill that made this a regular school district just like any other school district, rural school district, and they have a school here for the inmates and it's compulsory that they go to school up to a certain grade. Just like it is out in the free world where they have truant officers make you go to school, they make the inmates go to school till they get to the equivalent of eighth grade, something like that. But from there on it's their own choice whether to go or whether to not to go. And now they have better recreation programs. They have different groups come in here and sing to them, put on programs, things like that. Have a gym over there with basketball. In fact, they had a tournament over at Star City week before last and inmates went over and played basketball just like any other independent team. They have a lot better show than they used to have.

But I said it before and I'll say it now: you got a good rehabilitation program here, but there's no way to rehabilitate a man unless he wants to be. If he has it in his heart and his mind that he's gonna be a thief, he's gonna be a thief. I talk to a lot of the boys. I talked to one the other day about his condition, said he ought to straighten up. He said he wanted to be a thief, he liked being a thief, that he enjoyed it. I couldn't see it myself. He's been gone about a month and I understand he's in jail again and on his way back. So that's just the way it goes.

Some guys get in here, do their time, you never hear from them any more. Find their way back in society and make a go. I know men been in here and gone out and got in business, doing real well, making a good living. Others go out, they can't make it, come back again. You got to have that "want to" to do it. You can't do it for 'em, got to do it themself.

You worked under Murton, didn't you?

Yeah, I worked under him all the time he was here. I don't know; he was writing a book all the time he was here.

You think that was one of the reasons he was here?

I don't know that, it was 'way above me. But I do know

that the days when he was writing his book in the morning you couldn't have an audit with him, you couldn't talk to him. He'd have a sign up on his door, "Do not disturb." When he was superintendent here. You couldn't get in and see him at times he be writing his book.

I think—now I don't know—but I think he came here just tryin' to write that book and gain fame. That's what I really think he's tryin' to do. In other words, he's looking forward to leaving and making money off that book he's writing.

You were with him the day he dug up the bodies.

Yeah, he had me dig 'em up. Told me to go down there in the corner of that pasture, little sink there, a hole, told me to dig into it and see what I could find. I said, "I know what's in there already: some graves."

He says, "Just dig 'em up and see what you can find."

I said, "Yes, sir."

I went down there and started digging and his right-hand man come running and hollering, "Stop! Stop!" all alarmed.

I said, "What's the matter?"

"Press is not here yet."

I said, "Oh."

And then they came in a few minutes with three movie cameras set up, three news medias. He stopped me before I got the skeletons dug up until they got there. All three of them, CBS, NBC, and ABC, all three were there.

One of those guys told me they had it in New York next morning at eight o'clock on the streets in the paper. They flew it to Memphis and Atlanta and up to New York that night and had it on the press the next morning about the bodies being dug up down here.

Did you know they were there all along?

Oh, yeah, we knew they were there. It was an old cemetery there. Long time ago, used to be when an inmate come in here, a lot of time their people didn't know where they were, see. You take fifty or seventy-five years ago, Fort Smith or Texarkana, that was a long way from here then, you know. Somebody come down here and get caught in trouble some way, why, there wasn't no way to know where their people were. Lot of 'em didn't have people. The state'd have to bury them. Had the cemetery and would lay 'em in the grave down there.

And didn't they keep records in those days?

I don't know about the records, if there's any records about them or not. But they buried them down there anyway.

Murton was trying to make it appear they was murdered and put there, but that wasn't the case at all. They wasn't murdered and put there. They was just people that died and were buried there.

We had a incident here two years ago where an inmate died and his people wouldn't claim him. The state had to bury him.

Where'd they put him?

Pine Bluff. I believe they have a cemetery now for people that don't have any home or people. Pine Bluff or Little Rock. I believe it's Pine Bluff where he was put away.

Who's the best superintendent you've been under here?

Well, I couldn't say. 'Cause all seven of 'em been good to

me, I ain't gonna lie about it. A place like this, if you go along and do your work, do it right, for the good of the institution, you can get along with any of 'em. At least I found it like that. I came in nine years ago. I hired out to work, I needed a job. I went to work at two-fifty a month. I worked fourteen nights, was off one. Off two days a month, to be exact. Long hours—twelve hours a night—as I was telling you a while ago. It wasn't a case of wanting to work back in those days; it was a case of having to work.

How come you quit farming?

Just like everything else: if you're not a pretty good-sized farmer you just can't make it these days. Cost of living's so high, equipment's so high, and I just went to work for them here.

It was kind of fascinating for me, this type of work.

Farming was just out of reason, it's so high now, 'less you got a lot of land. Gotta have volume to do anything now.

I love it. Don't know why, but I do. It's nine years and I just like it better all the time.

I know 'most all the inmates. I don't know, I don't look at them as prisoners. Working with 'em and around 'em, it's just a bunch a fellas to me. I just go on workin'. 'Most all of 'em respect me. Kind of old anyway and I don't have any trouble out of 'em.

I have writ one disciplinary in the last three years. Just one. Told him what I wanted done. I expect him to go on and do it, I don't stand around hollerin' and screamin' at him all the time. If he don't do it, I take other measures, but most of the time a guy like that, you tell him what you want done, he'll go on and do it for you.

The last time I was here you were working at the sally-port gate.

Yeah, I was just temporary there. See, they got me classed as utility officer. I tell 'em, I do what nobody else wants to do. Like this job here, this is a relief job. The boy that was here in the hog lot quit, he resigned, and I'm just here temporarily in his place until they replace him with somebody else. Next week I might be at the gin or chicken house or out in the field or wherever they need me to relieve somebody. Just utility.

We have what they call a utility squad. Usually work anywhere from eight to ten men. They just do odd jobs around the farm. Building bridges, repairing places. We get quite a few old buildings outside to tear down, out in the free world. I do a lot of that—tearing down buildings, stuff like that, you know. They'll give us the material to tear them down. Lot of brick buildings, we'll salvage whatever we can out of it.

When I first got here, I worked from August to April and the following spring I took the plow squads. We plowed with mules then. Very few tractors—had them just to do the breakin'. Did all the cultivating with mules. I took the mule squads then, handled the mules and the inmates. Had about seventy-five to a hundred teams of mules. Plowed every day. That's a lot of 'em. That "Twenty-team Mule Borax" on TV—that wouldn't even start what we had.

We had lots of plowing, did lots of plowing with those mules.

This was a pretty rough place in those days.

It was. It was pretty rough. I was raised about four miles from here, so I been around it all my life, see. They used to kick 'em around pretty good back in the old days. You ought to talk to a lot of the old inmates here now—they was here then. They still hangin' around.

After all is said and done, it's a prison, and a man comes here to do his time and he can do it one of two ways. He can do it the hard way, day by day, or he can come in, act right, do his work as best he can, keep his business straight, get early parole, and leave here. Then it's up to him whether or not he's coming back.

But nine times out of ten—well, I won't say nine times out of ten, either, but seventy-five percent of 'em will go on and straighten up and make it, see. The others come back.

Tommy: ". . . you go down there and haul their goddamned heads. . . ."

Most American prisons use a convict management system not unlike the Kapo system in Nazi concentration camps: for special privileges, selected inmates do most of the day-to-day brutalization of their fellows. Tommy had such a job.

Let me run down to you about this floorwalker job I've got in here.

The second day I come in here this happened. They've got building tenders and they've got floorwalkers. They have got the authority from the man up there to just run shit on anybody they want to.

They told me when I took this floorwalker job, "You go down there, you go down there and haul their goddamned heads. Drag 'em up that yard desk, we'll take care of them, don't worry about a thing, we'll back you a hundred percent. . . ." They tell you all this shit. They want you to come down here and kick ass, man.

All right: the second day I'm here I come back from the photo lab. I had that fingerprint shit on my fingers. I'm in there washing my hands and this building tender tells me, "Boy, I'm sure glad you got back."

I said, "Why is that?"

He says, "I thought I was gonna have to grab me one of them mops. But you can get your ass out there on one of them now."

I said, "All right." I kept on washing my hands. So I got through washing my hands and I walked back to my bed and got my razor. I needed a shave. The Man had told me to shave while I was up there. He caught me out in the hall and told me to get the whiskers off. So I came back and I'm shaving. He goes and gets two of his partners.

They drive up on me in the bathroom and say, "Hey, Slim."

I say, "Yeah?"

They say, "You gonna get your ass out here on this mop?"

I say, "Yeah, I'll come out there and help you mop whenever I get through shaving."

They say, "No. You get your ass out here now."

I says, "Look, man, the Man told me to come in here and shave and I'll come out there and help you when I get through."

They say, "Oh, you a bad sonofabitch, huh?"

I said, "No. Now look: I'm doing too much time to be

fucking with you jokers. Now you go on and quit fucking with me and when I get through here I'll help out. I ain't trying to run no game on you. Yesterday I worked all fucking day in this barracks. I ain't goin' up behind this shit, I don't want no trouble, but I ain't going to take no shit."

One says, "I tell you what, you motherfucker, you be going down to Seven Barracks when you get through here and I got friends there and we'll just stick your ass off in the infirmary."

I said, "No, man, you ain't stickin' me no goddamned place. You gonna threaten me with the goddamned infirmary, and I'll stick your ass in the goddamned infirmary." I said, "You fuck with me, I'll run a piece of steel through you, you motherfucker."

So I start on him and this friend of his comes around behind me, this other friend comes beside of me and he says, "We might just stick you in the infirmary now."

So I just knocked him plumb out of the shitter. Then they all just scattered, man. This barber—I did time with his brother in another state—this big black dude up there, he grabs this one, and I hit this other one, knocked him over this box.

They go down and holler, "Fight!" and all this shit. "Fight! These motherfuckers are crazy in here." So they come down with the sticks and they take me and this one guy up to the yard desk.

They say, "Get the witnesses on this." The witnesses come down and they're the guys I'm fighting with. They say, "This man, we asked him to come out and help us mop and he told us that he didn't have to do no goddamned mopping, that he was doing twenty-five years and we better not be fucking with him," and all this shit. And this guy, the one I hit first, his story was that he was walking out of the bathroom and I hit him in the back of the head, he didn't even know what I hit him for, he ain't done a goddamned thing to me.

I go up to the disciplinary court—I'm the only one that goes to disciplinary court. They keep me on Max five days. I go to disciplinary court and they reduce me to class three. They say I can't get out of class three until I get me a supervisor.

What they do is they put these guys in these barracks with all that bullshit in their heads: "You do what you want and we'll back you," and all this shit. I get tired of this goddamned shit and I get into it with some more guys over here and it ain't my fault again, man. And the major's clerk is pickin' up on what's going down, so I tell him, "Man, you go down there and get me one of these floorwalker jobs. I'm getting tired of this fucken shit. I'm going to get into it with a motherfucker and he's going to go up there and lie on me and I'm going to lose my class. Shit."

So he says, "OK."

They haul me up there and they say, "We hear you don't mind mixing it up."

I say, "I don't mind it. I don't like no unnecessary trouble."

"Will you get down there and hull them heads out?"

I said, "Yeah, I'll go down there."

They said, "All right, we'll get your class back for you and we'll back you up a hundred percent" and all this shit.

I come down here and I don't run any games on anybody and if I catch any of them floorwalkers running any games on anybody I'll knock fire from their ass. I can't see the way they got this system set up, man, you know? And the only way to do it, I figure, was to get me one of these jobs to keep these motherfuckers from running over these other poorassed motherfuckers.

You don't do no wrong if you're a floorwalker or building tender. You get in some kind of hassle with another inmate, they're gonna write disciplinaries on both of you, but they never take any action on the floorwalker or building tender. The inmate who got into it, he rides the beef. He's automatically wrong.

A floorwalker can do head-strumming a lot more easily than the guards can.

That's what they use us for.

That's the general idea: to do their ass-whippin' for them. If you're gonna kick ass, you're gonna kick ass for us.

C. Robert Sarver, former Arkansas prison commissioner: "Flies, mosquitoes and vermin of all sorts . . ."

"With the removal of the strap and other methods of corporal punishment to keep prisoners in line, you had to depend on wit rather than cruelty and brute force to make them do things. It became a matter with the staff and I just had to spend each day and each hour hoping that nothing would go wrong, and when it did go wrong, trying to call on your wits to keep it under control.

"I recall that I had never seen anything worse for a prison setting. Flies, mosquitoes and vermin of all sorts were running around during my first visit to Cummins and Tucker in August.

"One inmate was covered entirely with a sheet as he slept and the sheet just looked like a polka-dotted sheet from the mass of flies and mosquitoes that were crawling on it. I recall the odor in the dining room that would make any kind of meal unpalatable. There was a terrible lack of staff, which hit a low point in November 1960 when we had to lay off so many because we couldn't pay their salaries." [Quoted in the *Arkansas Gazette,* May 2, 1971]

Dirty Harry: "The sorriest people on earth is right here."

At the sally-port gate one day, someone named Kid said he thought having inmate guards was a good idea because it was "an opportunity for nine or ten different inmates to have a job like that where they're respected, not just something low." Two older convicts standing nearby guffawed. One said:

Let me correct you in that one respect: you're not respected by the free people or the convicts either when you take that gun up in that tower. The very goddamned day that something goes wrong they'll bust you right out of that sonofabitch and throw you right back in that barracks.

They don't respect you at all. That don't mean a damned

thing. You're a sorry sonofabitch either way they look at it. Now I don't know who filled your head full of foolish ideas, but I can tell you something: when you walk into the chow hall the first thing they'll say is "Look at that sorry sonofabitch. He's out there with that gun keepin' us here." They don't respect you in your fucken job. If they thought they could, they'd try to get out if they could do it. Any position you hold here—like the one you have on that count book—to them people you're a sorry motherfucker. You always remember that.

And when you get out on them streets, you be walkin' down the street and one of them stinkin' bastards out there, the first thing he'll say when he sees you and has somebody with him, "I know that old thing from down yonder. Stay away from that sonofabitch. He's a sorry motherfucker. He'll call the law."

I know the way they think.

I'll tell you something: always remember there ain't a one of these motherfuckers here doing your time. That judge give it to you. I can't do it and can't a swinging dick here that can do it for you. Do your goddamned time the best way you can and get out of this ratty bastard. 'Cause the sorriest people on earth is right here. The worst goddamned scum.

I've worked the state of Florida down around those winos, where they lug goddamned watermelons and pick oranges all day and drink wine. But they wouldn't run and call the law on each other. They'd get out there and fight and they'd sleep in the goddamned palmettos, but you never would see one of them say, "That other one snitched on me." No. Why? They have respect for each other.

These sonofabitches here don't even respect their mama. When she comes to see them, if she don't leave them a dollar or two they cuss her. The sonofabitches, they'll tell you up in that barracks, over sixty percent of them, "The only reason I ever see mama is so I can get a dollar or two." Or "Boy, I sure be glad when my wife get here Saturday or Sunday," whenever she supposed to be here. And then when she don't be here, "I bet that goddamned long-cock sonofabitch is out there fucking somebody." And he gonna write an old sarcastic letter and two weeks later he's gonna write her a good letter and try to get her back down here 'cause he wants a dollar or two.

You got some people here, boy, that don't even love their mammy.

Assistant Superintendent Michaels: ". . . we didn't ask for you to come. . ."

I first met Michaels a decade earlier when I was doing research in Texas prisons and he was working for a man convicts said was the toughest, meanest, most honest, and fairest warden in that part of the country: Carl Luther McAdams, nicknamed "The Bear" or "Beartracks." The Bear brought Michaels up in the prison business, all the way from field guard to field major in Texas. When T. D. Hutto moved from Texas to take over the Arkansas prison system, Michaels was one of the men he brought along. He said Michaels was young enough to be able to adjust to the very different Arkansas situation, but knowledgeable and tough enough to handle the problems of administrative chaos the new staff faced. The first problem was the lack of civilian guards. Michaels, more than any other member of the new staff, was responsible for handling the changeover from a convict guard system.

Few convicts realized how young Michaels was. For most of his career, they've all been older than he. For a long time, his face was the most deceptive factor: all those years in the fields gave him a weathered look, one shared with so many of those southwestern farmers documented in the FSA photographs of Dorothea Lange and Walker Evans, men somewhere between thirty and fifty, anywhere between thirty and fifty.

Since he's come in from the field and taken over the job of assistant superintendent of Cummins, his features have softened. I asked him questions about his job.

I think the hardest part for me has been not to have barrel vision. You know me, you know my past in Texas. Sometimes I catch myself kind of paralleling this system with the Texas system, which is wrong, 'cause even though I think the Texas system was good, I feel as though there were some things in it could be changed, that would be better.

And I try not to have barrel vision. I try to look at both sides. I try not to be so hard-shell conservative, you know,

that I can't think outside of that. And sometimes the hours and the problems—the inmate problems *and* the employee problems—they get so great you begin not to think, you just react in a pattern that you're used to. I think this is wrong and this is my hardest part: not reacting in a pattern.

And training officers. I was not used to that. I was used to having a guy come to work for me that had been trained, maybe been working for the system for several years and then come to the field. That was Texas. Here, I was working with guys that never worked in the building, just came to the field.

I didn't have *any* field officers. There was no such person. They had some guys that had been working here I think since July in the field, but they didn't have any supervision. At the time they didn't have anybody that had ever really worked a squad before.

When I first came here, we had three or four hoe squads as such. And we still had three longlines. As we progressed along and I got officers trained to where they could work with a squad, then we would break down another part of another longline and just gradually work until we got 'em all broke down.

I had no problem with the longlines. The biggest trouble was with an inmate with a weapon telling another inmate what to do. I don't care for that.

Was there much resistance among inmates about getting rid of those convict guards?

No, they were for it, they were more for it really than

probably we were. They wanted it done faster because they felt it was wrong, which I agreed with. Even though we still have inmate guards on the towers—twelve of them—we closely scrutinize them. Their role has been greatly reduced from what it used to be. They just do the job mostly watching, don't let anybody get over the fence or escape or attempt to escape. This is about all, whereas in the past they had actually run the place. I don't like that whatsoever.

I think another thing which scared me to death when I come up here was the weapons that they kept in the building, you know, the gun cages and stuff like that. It was a great relief to me to see them taken out of the building.

This is the first prison I've been where I've seen guns in the building.

I think violence begets violence in a way. A show of force is good in certain situations, you know, when you *have* to show force. But violence begets violence. If you got guns in here, that's violent. You're gonna have it. And the way they were using the weapons, shooting them and all, was wrong. So they really just kind of aggravated the situation; it didn't have any protective value to it.

As we gained free-world employees with a little bit of training, we began to slowly take over. It took awhile.

This is not to say that some inmates can't handle a little bit of authority if it's given to them. In fact, I think it's good sometimes to give a guy a little bit of authority, an inmate. But also have it on a checks-and-balance system where he can't use this authority just ruthlessly. You can watch.

I think possibly in the last five years, the hardest type of individual for me to handle is the—not young offender, not eighteen or nineteen—but the guy that's twenty-one, twenty-two, twenty-three years old that's been raised in a permissive setting and brought up in that. And probably the institution is the first real confrontation he's had with any regulation of his life. He's bitter when he comes here because he feels that the Establishment put him here, and the Establishment *is* here.

And we try to put over to him that we didn't tell you to come to the penitentiary, we didn't ask for you to come, don't consider us like that. Consider this: you got the time, the judge committed you here, and the more open-minded you are about accepting things, the quicker you'll progress inside the institution itself as far as better jobs, class, good time, and things like that.

But I find these people are a problem because they really don't understand. And no matter how you try or what you say will they admit that you may be partially right.

What you're saying is they won't say they're responsible for why they're here. If a man won't do that or can't do that or doesn't think that, what can you possibly do with him while he's here?

Only hope that in the process of his time and growing up . . . We were talking the other night about the "burnout factor." You hope that he grows up. You hope that he may eventually find an officer or an employee that he will identify with, a stable person. You know, you and I were talking that probably the best rehabilitation process is a one-to-one basis. Officer to an inmate. And you hope that maybe somewhere along the line he will identify.

And rehabilitation: as far as that goes, there is no way—I firmly believe there is no way— You can offer a man program and program and program, counseling after counseling, but until he makes up his mind nothing is going to happen. He can sit there and say, "Yeah, you're right. Yeah, you're OK and I understand and I know I'm wrong." But the greatest psychiatrist on the face of the earth, people that deal with people's minds, cannot really tell you for sure, a hundred percent positive, whether or not this man is being truthful with you or is putting you on.

When this guy makes up his mind, "Well, I'm gonna change. Here's a little something in my life that, yeah, I'm a little wrong," or maybe not necessarily that he's wrong, "Maybe I kind of goofed up here. I really knew better than that. I won't do it any more."

This—the burnout factor—is probably the biggest thing. You just hope that this guy that's twenty-one or twenty-two that hadn't really rationalized before in his life will maybe rationalize things into a more middle spectrum than he now is. He doesn't look at things as either left or right but begins to maybe look at left and right and compare, you know, and make a judgment or comparison or grouping. No one can say that left is right or right is right; you take some of left and some of right and you make your own decision as to what is right.

You talk about a guy that's institutionalized: somewhere along the line, even in the institution, he's going to reach a point where he's going to have to make a decision. Just a minor decision. Say you put a guy in the laundry and here comes a shirt through that's torn and he's on the press. He can just press it and send it back in. Or he can take the man's shirt over to the repair section, have it repaired, and take it back and then press it. I think that inside you can watch a guy—because once he gets out of this society, this controlled society, he has to make those little nickel/dime decisions that every guy does on the street every day as to whether to get up and go to work: "Really, am I sick enough not to work?" or "Do I really need to get a drink now or should I wait?" This sort of thing. You can watch these little nickel/dime decisions that he makes in here. And you can say, "The guy's making progress."

I think a good supervisor can begin to make this guy make these decisions by telling him, "Hey, don't just press this shirt. It don't take a minute longer to toss it over and let the guy sew it and bring it back."

And after a while the guy says, "Well, that's what the Man wants me to do, that's OK. I'll just make that decision myself."

At first, every time he gets one that's torn he'll say, "Mr. Supervisor, do you want me to get this sewn up?"

Finally, supervisor says, "Look, does it need sewing?"

"Yeah."

"Then get it sewed." Then he begins to make those decisions. And in a small way he begins to pull away from being institutionalized.

I don't think anybody likes an institutionalized convict.

They're easy as hell to handle in the institution. They're no problem. But I think even administrators don't like an institutionalized con. They like a guy that's not institutionalized but he cares enough about doing his time to follow the rules and regulations but yet to open his mind up and begin to explore and think for himself a little bit. I think in a system like this, the more help an inmate wants here, the more he can get, if he just asks. He's gonna have to ask.

Then you get a guy, he constantly makes decisions for himself that are contrary to the policies or the rules and you got to slow him down. You say, "Look, you got to be a little more rational about things. Here's a rule saying you don't walk down the hall with your shirt off. Put your shirt on."

"Well, I don't wear my shirt at home."

"Well, that's OK, that's fine, but this is the rule. Put your shirt on."

I'll tell you what the shirt's all about. Six weeks ago I put out a rule: "All inmates will come down the hall with proper footwear and a shirt." In the past, there hadn't been this rule and they came down the hall in sweatshirts, T-shirts, half-shoes, shower shoes. I told the security staff, "Don't write anybody up for a week or two. If you see a guy coming down, say, 'Get your shirt,' or 'Get your shoes.' Don't say, 'You're not coming in here to eat.' Say, 'Put your shirt on and come back in here and eat.'" Took us about three days and nobody showed up in the hall without shirt on and shoes on. No hassle, no problems.

They really wanted somebody to say, "You got to be dressed right." You tell a guy, "Look: even though you're an inmate in an institution, you still got to care a little bit about something. You got to have a little self-pride. And by your dress and by the way you act you can have it."

The small things in here amount to big things, big decisions. And people in outside society don't think that.

I think possibly a lot of people come back to institutions because society won't accept them. We tell ourselves, "Oh, yeah, poor guy's been in the penitentiary for five years and we're really gonna help him." But I think if the truth were known, a guy gets called an ex-con for so long and has a gut feeling there and says, "Well, hell, I'm just gonna do what these people want me to do." Because he's shook, he's frustrated, and he's scared anyway.

I think society turns around and says to us, "Well, you didn't do a good job of rehabilitating him." Also I think society doesn't give a guy a fair shake either. Coming out.

And where and when that place in time be reached when they give that guy a fair shake and people in institutions give him the type of rehabilitative help that he needs, who knows: he might be able to make it.

You know, every state tries something different, but the recidivism rate is about the same. So what does work? What *really* does work? I think two things: burnout and education. You don't see but very few people with masters' degrees in institutions.

4. Black and White

There is no prison in the United States in which one does not find in exacerbated form the ethnic and racial problems that have so convulsed all our urban centers in the past several decades. That is because prison populations are disproportionately drawn from the poor and uneducated, and it is in those groups that the ethnic and racial problems are most severe.

The several newspaper articles and interview excerpts that follow illustrate aspects of racial problems in the Arkansas prisons over a four-year period. The important shift, one paralleled across the country, is from a situation in which minorities battled majorities (blacks versus whites here) to a situation in which the minorities directed their anger against the prison administrators and the prison system itself.

It is obvious from these statements that Arkansas inmates were several years behind the political awareness of their northern counterparts. It was the same in these years in Texas, Mississippi, Louisiana, and the other southern prisons: it seemed for a long time that the events in New York and California and New Jersey had never happened.

There might seem to be a curious discrepancy here: the civil rights movement of the 1960s occurred in the South, but the South remains far more conservative politically than the North. Southern discrimination took institutional and legislated forms, and it is easier to demonstrate against segregated bus depots and restaurants than against the more subtle—but no less pervasive—forms of discrimination in northern cities. There is no reason to expect convicts to handle these patterns differently from everyone else.

Associate Superintendent Cecil Boren: ". . . kill the first one that lights a match. . . ."

The second rebellion by Cummins State Prison Farm inmates during November occurred yesterday afternoon when fist fights broke out between black and white prisoners.

On November 2 when eight inmates took over the prison's isolation unit and held six hostages, including state Correction Commissioner Robert Sarver and Cummins Superintendent Bill Steed, at gunpoint for up to 12½ hours before surrendering [sic].

Trouble was brewing at Cummins between black and white inmates for some time, according to one prison official. Inmate barracks at Cummins were integrated April 4 on orders from federal Judge J. Smith Henley of Little Rock.

Sarver said early today that the situation was "very tense." He said the disturbance had evolved into "black versus white."

Sarver, Steed and other prison officials spent the night in counsel with the inmates, but according to Associate Superintendent Cecil Boren negotiations were not successful.

Sarver said the fights broke out yesterday as the inmates were coming in from the long line for lunch. He said both the white group and the black group were making a number of demands, including demands to go back to segregated housing quarters and segregated work details. . . .

Boren . . . blamed the trouble on black inmates. He said

the whites had been cooperative but that the blacks were "unruly" and intent on "burning this place down." Boren said he would "kill the first one that lights a match" because he was going to "protect the state's property." [*Pine Bluff Commercial,* November 21, 1970]

C. Robert Sarver, former prison commissioner: "The troopers worked them and they whacked them. . . ."

"There was only 16 of us there at the time it all began.

"Cecil Boren, chief of security, came up, his eyes full of tears. Someone had let go with a tear gas bomb in A barracks. The fighting had almost become barracks-wide. Not quite, but it had reached the point in the middle of the barracks where officers could not go in without weapons. So the tear gas grenade was thrown in there.

"The gas began filling up the whole building. We had gas in our eyes until dawn.

"It had gotten so out of hand that Bill Steed and I radioed for the State Police at 8:20 p.m. . . .

"At that point we were grouping and trying to decide what steps to take. We knew what we had to do.

"We removed all trusties who were in the guard towers and put troopers in the towers.

"I went back to the dining hall and talked to the white inmates there to find out for sure just who the rabble-rousers were. It didn't take long to find out.

"There were some blacks working in the kitchen at that time preparing food. They were in very small number and there were 70 of the whites in the back end of the dining hall. I found out who the leaders were and I started to leave, back out.

"A fight broke out between a black and a white inmate. The whole white group started moving toward the fight. I ran back and screamed at the inmate, the white, and told him to stand where he was. The black came out and stood by me.

"About that time another fight broke out on the other side of the kitchen. The white group started moving in that direction.

"By that time things were being thrown through the air and they were screaming and raising hell. You cannot imagine the things flying through the air.

"The blacks and I began moving toward the door as fast as we could. Most of them were crawling on the floor. That's when I got knocked down to the floor: someone just ran over me trying to get to the door.

"We got outside. I wanted tear gas in there badly because I was afraid that they would tear up the kitchen. Then we would have a problem feeding the men.

"About that time a group of state troopers came down the hall with their shotguns. They went into the dining hall, cocked their shotguns and that was the end of it, as far as the dining room incident was concerned.

"We then herded them into the gymnasium and cleaned out the dining hall. From that point on, the State Police were in charge and it never got out of control again. They left Monday morning without firing a shot.

"The troopers banged around a good many. When they said 'Move,' they meant 'Move!!' If a man didn't move, then they moved him. . . .

"I think they did things that had to be done," Sarver said of the troopers. "I'm glad our staff didn't have to do them. We have to live there and we just cannot do those things.

"I'm not so sure that all of those things were absoluetly necessary, but they got the situation under control without undue bodily harm to very many people. Most of them who got banged around deserved it. They needed it.

"It was a doubtful situation, and even passive resistance in a doubtful situation is tantamount to manifested violence, even though it may be in a passive manner. You cannot have that kind of behavior in that kind of situation.

"The people who always get hurt are the inmates. Inevitably, some staff members may get hurt. We wanted to avoid that, so the troopers were banging around the ones who were there, and everyone else around. That is what has to be done.

"I'm sure there were some innocent men who got clobbered, men who weren't even involved. Again, in that kind of situation, you can't discriminate too much between the good and bad inmates.

"The troopers worked them and they whacked them around if they didn't." [Quoted in the *Arkansas Gazette,* May 4, 1971]

Ervin Lacy: "A lot of problems could be resolved if all cooperate together."

Ervin Lacy, a black inmate serving a life sentence for rape from Phillips County, testified that conditions had improved recently for those who practice the Muslim faith.

The group is now allowed three rather than two meetings monthly, he said, and has been given a better, quieter place to hold their meetings. The improvements came about after requesting help from Lockhart and other officials, Lacy testified. Remaining problems that deal with permission to meet on a weekly basis, conduction of education courses and observance of dietary bans on pork and other food items are being considered by the officials, he said.

Lacy concluded his testimony with a plea that Henley consider giving the Muslim religion an opportunity to reform the Arkansas prison system, on the grounds that "a lot of problems could be resolved if all cooperate together." Adherents of the Muslim faith have ceased to commit new crimes, Lacy said, and "everything else has been tried and failed." Progress has been made in reforming the prisons, Lacy said, but more funds are needed to better operate the institutions and the court hearings on conditions cost money. [*Pine Bluff Commercial,* December 20, 1972]

Associate Superintendent Cecil Boren: ". . . any man could judge any other man."

Despite a prison population that is 48 per cent black, Boren testified, he never considered the lack of a black officer on the disciplinary court as any problem until recently. "I have the last couple of weeks," Boren continued, as inmates complained in federal court earlier that they felt an all-white court discriminated against black inmates. For a period a black chaplain sat on the court, but he declined to vote for fear of jeopardizing his relationship with inmates, Boren testified.

Although he declined to assert he never discriminated in issuing judgments during his 4.5 years in charge of disciplinary court, Boren said he believed "any man could judge any other man." [*Pine Bluff Commerical,* January 6, 1973]

Superintendent A. L. Lockhart: "never abused any inmate."

A. L. Lockhart, superintendent at Cummins State Prison Farm, testified that he never struck or verbally abused any inmate, black or white. He also denied offering to arrange to drop charges of escape against Lyndale Walker in exchange for not testifying last year in a similar hearing in federal court on prison conditions. Several inmates earlier had testified that Lockhart participated in striking them or calling them names, and Walker claimed that Lockhart bargained for dropping the escape charge with his silence.

Since 1971 no felony charges have been filed against escapees, Lockhart testified, and instead the offense is handled through the prison disciplinary court. This was decided as a way to handle the problem without incurring court costs of taking them to Star City for an appearance in Lincoln County Circuit Court, he said.

. . . Since the hearings before Federal Judge J. Smith Henley of Little Rock a year ago, Lockhart testified, two officers have been discharged for brutality to an inmate, and a third officer involved was suspended briefly and not allowed to return to work. . . . Another officer named Kelly was fired shortly after he was employed for shoving an inmate too roughly during a general shakedown, Lockhart testified.

The three who were dismissed for their involvement in beating Montgomery were "some of our better employees," Lockhart said, several of whom had been recommended for promotions. [*Pine Bluff Commercial,* January 6, 1973]

Willie: "This institution . . . is going to explode one day. . . ."

The other night, what really happened, the white building tender down in Eight Barracks had been jumping on black inmates time and time again and nobody been doing nothing about it. The administration hadn't been doing nothing about it. This happened about three or four times, different times. And so last Thursday, the white inmate had jumped on a black inmate again, the same building tender, but this time some of the blacks didn't go for it. They stopped it.

Administrators like Major Fisher knew about this incident and most of the time he tells the white building tenders, "Go ahead and do what you want to them niggers and you don't have to worry about nothin' because we won't do nothin' about it." So some of the blacks got together and they stopped it and rebelled against it. They got tired of being jumped on.

Some of the Muslim brothers told some of them not to get involved with it, that they'd try to handle it another way. So when they came with the guns and stuff they wanted the Muslim brothers to break their necks and run out there, but they wouldn't run out. They waited for each brother to come out before they decided to come out of the barracks. They wasn't going to leave out of the barracks without all the brothers leaving out of the barracks at the same time 'cause they were bound by the laws of Islam to stick together.

So this is what happened down in Eight Barracks last week.

How many Muslims are there?

In this institution? Approximately thirty-five.

How many were Muslims on the street?

Approximately two.

You can look around. We don't have but one black officer in this whole institution, that lieutenant. There's two black field officers. That black officer that works up front is in the Rehab, but that's not part of back here. We don't have but one black lieutenant. You look around, you got about ten lieutenants, two white majors, about six white captains, and, shit, so many white sergeants it's a shame. But none of 'em blacks. We ain't got no black captain and no black chaplain.

A dude walk around here in class one or class two for a year, a year and a half, then all of a sudden him and a warden might get into an argument, and the warden turn around and write a disciplinary on him. Shit: that year and a half of work he did in class one or class two all went for nothing because the disciplinary court gonna take it all away. Put him in class four where he can't earn his class, so actually he's just walkin' around here working for nothing. Shit. This here is a hell of a threat over an inmate's head.

This is my third term down here. First time was in 1968. It's worse now than it ever was. You didn't have to worry then about them poppin' a inferiority complex towards you because they knew where it was, they knew they was running everything so they had no reason. But these free-world men running it down here now, they cause the inferiority complex. Half of 'em got a high school education and they get against a guy like me that do have a education so they heap abuse and keep me locked up in the hole. There's wardens walking around here twenty-one, nineteen, twenty-two years old and I got to say "Yes, sir," to them and I'm the same age they is. I'm twenty-one and I got to say "Yes, sir," to each one of them.

Since the first time down here, I've managed to accept it just as I would living in a house with my brothers and sisters.

How old were you then?

Fifteen.

Did you go to Tucker?

Yes. Then when I came back, I was sixteen. I went over to Tucker, got into a whole lot of stuff over there. Instigating a sit-down, jumping on a warden, and they sent me back over here and tried to intimidate me over here. I refused to be intimated over here.

Ever since then it has been the same way: I refuse to bow down to them and they refuse to give me any ground. So I've just had a war with every administration that come through here.

Some of the inmates here looks up to me because they know what kind of inmate I am: I don't suck ass with Mr. Lockhart or any of them.

I'd like to say that every writ I've filed in the institution, I've never told a lie about it.

I feel blacks shouldn't take up guns [as inmate guards]. I don't like the idea. I really don't like it. I feel that the Man is using them. Because every time somebody run off or something happens, he snatch them off the tower and put them in the hole. They're an inmate just like me. You gonna shoot a man for just running off at the fence or running away from here?

First of all, he's in a slavery camp, that's what this is, mostly a slavery camp. You can't blame a person who'd want to get away from a slavery camp.

I have seen many places and I have heard of many places and this is the first hellhole that I ever seen that is the way it is ran here at Cummins institution. 'Cause this is slavery.

The money that they make in this institution, in a self-supporting institution, this should be the best-fed institution, the best-fed inmates in the United States. They have this so-called thing, a trick thing called the Inmate Council. All the officials, I feel, are making money. Because the inmates aren't getting nothing. They get two packs of tobacco, two packs of Tops, a week, and one razor blade. A *week*. Now, you go down the hall and if you ain't shaved, they write you up. But they only give you one razor blade.

This institution, I feel, is going to explode one day and I feel it's going to be a terrible explosion. I can see, how you say, I can see the storm before it hit. It's coming. It's building up. You having little incidents happening now, little riots, little small fights, but it's building up. You can see it's coming, it's coming. The pressure.

5. Disciplinary Actions

"Unusual Occurrences"

Somewhere in the middle of the thick statistical reports that make up the Cummins Monthly Report packet (details of prison population movements, expenditures, farm sales, acreage allocations, equipment acquisition, medical supply utilization) is a small prose section detailing data not amenable to numerical accounting. The section consists of short narratives giving the backgrounds of major disciplinary actions and what the prison system refers to as "unusual occurrences."

In some ways, the disciplinary reports and the "unusual occurrence" narratives can be considered the lunatic edge of prison life: one finds documented here only behavior extraordinary enough to involve the official workings of the prison bureaucracy. Like most large institutions, prisons try to handle informally as much pathology as possible, for irregular disturbances require kinds of paperwork that bureaucracies traditionally dislike.

And that is why the little narratives are important documents. They reveal something that observation of normal life within the institution doesn't: the savage intensity of the frustration engendered by the situation, the unfocused anger of the convicts erupting in terrible self-destructive fury. There is no way a convict can attack guards and hope to win, everyone knows that, and the fact that these eruptions occur anyway attests to the dimension of the rage. Six of the seven reports that follow are about convicts. One is about a guard: outrageous inability to behave rationally is not an aberration limited to the convicts.

On February 1st, Mr. James, Correctional Officer I, was making his round on Punitive Wing, East Building. As he passed Punitive Cells he found inmate Sullivan bent over and crying. Mr. James asked Sullivan what was wrong and Sullivan replied that he had stuck something up his rectum and asked Mr. James would he get a Doctor. There was cotton strown [sic] about the cell that had been torn out of the mattress to substantiate Sullivan's statement. Officer James immediately called Sgt. Fiddle, East Building Shift Supervisor, who in turn notified Mr. Lloyd, Medical Officer. Mr. Lloyd came to the East Building and examined Sullivan but could find no evidence of anything in his rectum. After consultation, the Officers opinion was that Sullivan had used stuffing cotton up his rectum as a subterfuge. A home made rope was found, made from torn sheets hanging from the bars in inmate Sullivan's cell, strongly suggesting that inmate Sullivan had attempted to hang himself. Officers removed inmate Sullivan's mattress, sheet, pants and jacket as a precautionary measure and placed inmate Sullivan back in his cell. Mr. Lloyd administered a Dolene and two Thorazine pills. This inmate was checked by East Building Officers every thirty minutes on a regular schedule. The medication took effect and there was no further incident with this inmate. Inmate Sullivan was transfered to the Tucker Unit, Feburary 14th.

While on duty in the East Building Sgt. Waring, Correctional Officer II, and Lt. Bowles, Shift Supervisor, were called back to the Punitive Wing by Mr. Smith, Correctional Officer. Upon arriving on Punitive Wing both

Officers were informed by Mr. Smith that inmate Harold who was on Administrative segregation had cut his wrist and stuck a piece of razor blade up his penis. Lt. Bowles ordered that inmate Harold be taken to the Infirmary where he was examined by Medical personnel. Inmate Harold was admitted to the infirmary for observation. An investigation was conducted by Officers of the East Building to determine where Harold had obtained the razor blade. It was the consensus of opinion that inmate Harold did not use a razor blade that was issued to inmates confined to Punitive Wing as it takes a special wrench to open the razor. Where Harold obtained the razor blade would be conjecture. As of this writing inmate Harold has been transferred to the State Hospital at Little Rock, Arkansas, and returned to the infirmary. Harold is scheduled to return to the hospital at Little Rock for further medical tests and final disposition of his case.

NOTE: Inmate Harold has a prior history of self-mutilation at this institution. Documented incident reports of this inmate's will reflect that when Harold is confined to the East Building for any disciplinary action his immediate reaction is to resort to self-mutilation. This inmate appears to do this in a retaliatory manner.

At approximately 11:45 A.M. on July 1, Sgt. Fiddle returned to Maximum Security with Inmate Charles after an interview with Mr. Hutto at the Main Building.

When Inmate Charles entered his cell, he placed his arms through the bars and covered the key slot in the door with his hands. Sgt. Fiddle tried to move his hands but Inmate Charles would not cooperate and suddenly shoved the door open, pinning Sgt. Fiddle against the wall. Inmate Charles then grabbed Sgt. Fiddle by the arm, tearing off his watch. Sgt. Fiddle hit Inmate Charles with his fist and knocked him back enough to get partially free, but Inmate Charles grabbed him by the shoulder and again pushed him back. Sgt. Fiddle then hit Inmate Charles with a slap-jack and knocked him to his knees. Only dazed, Inmate Charles got back up and Inmate Riley, the day porter, then jumped him from behind and attempted to aid Sgt. Fiddle. Inmate Charles broke away from Inmate Riley and Sgt. Fiddle again hit him with the slap-jack, knocking him to the floor. At this time, Sgt. Fiddle was able to move Inmate Charles into his cell and locked the door.

Captain Tower was called to Maximum Security and upon arrival, he escorted Inmate Murphy to the Infirmary to receive a tetanus shot. When Inmate Riley was returned to Maximum Security, Captain Tower was met by Mr. Boren. Inmate Charles was then handcuffed and escorted to the infirmary by Captain Tower and Mr. Boren. He was treated for a cut on his head and transferred to the Arkansas State Hospital for observation. Inmate Charles remains confined at the Arkansas State Hospital in Rogers Hall as of this writing.

At approximately 1945 hours on July 5, Sgt. Simpson and Sgt. Neill were making a routine check of the cells on the Punitive Wing of Maximum Security. Upon reaching Inmate McCarthy's cell, they observed that he had broken out the glass in the light fixture and scratched the door to his cell. Inmate McCarthy was removed from his cell and he became very violent, threatening to kill both officers. He was taken to the Quiet Cell and the door was closed at 1955 hours.

At 2145 hours, Mr. Boren proceeded to Maximum Security to release Inmate McCarthy from the Quiet Cell. As Mr. Boren opened the door, Inmate McCarthy stated that he was going to kill his field officer if ever given the chance. He also told Mr. Boren, "I better not live to get out of here or you will regret it." After this, Inmate McCarthy was placed back in his regular cell, with the continued threat to kill everyone involved. No force was used at any time during this incident.

On the morning of July 10, Officer Snow was assigned to #2 Hoe Squad, working in the cucumber field.

Officer Snow asked Inmate Wheeler back on his row to counsel with him. He asked Inmate Wheeler if he had any good time and what class he was in. Inmate Wheeler looked at him very belligerently and stated, "I don't give a fuck about any good time or my classification. I'm doing 21 years and there isn't any white mother-fucker going to tell me how to get down my row." He further stated, "I'm a bad son-of-a-bitch and I will get shitty with you." Inmate Wheeler then, without warning or cause, drew back and began to swing at Officer Snow. Realizing his intentions,

Officer Snow hit Inmate Wheeler in his own defense. A fight erupted and Inmate Wheeler's actions could not be controlled. He would not stop fighting and Officer Snow was forced to continue in his defense. During the fight, Officer Lucas arrived and attempted to aid Officer Snow. Inmate Wheeler then turned and struck Officer Lucas with his fists. Both officers finally managed to restrain Inmate Wheeler and then summoned for Lt. Becker. Inmate Wheeler was taken to the infirmary for treatment of minor cuts and received four stitches above his eye. He was then escorted to Maximum Security and placed in the Quiet Cell with the door remaining open.

At approximately 1530 hours, Major Fisher and Dr. Barber went to Maximum Security to counsel with Inmate Shay. As they approached his cell, they observed Inmate Shay lying on the floor. Major Fisher asked Inmate Shay to stand up, as they could not talk with him while he was lying down. Inmate Shay replied, "Piss on you." Major Fisher turned to walk away and Inmate Shay then told Dr. Walters, "I'm going to kill a warden and I'm not going to stay in this cell." Major Fisher and Dr. Barber then left without any further conversation.

At approximately 1830 hours, Sgt. Simpson discovered that Inmate Shay had torn out the light fixture in his cell and broken the glass in his cell door. Inmate Shay told Sgt. Simpson that he was going to tear down the entire cell if he was not permitted a cigarette. Sgt. Simpson called Major Fisher and was then instructed to place Inmate Shay in the

Quiet Cell. This was done at 1830 hours and the door remained open.

Inmate Gatlin was returning from work at approximately 2115 hours on the evening of July 24. As he entered the West Hall door, Officer Burns approached to shake down the inmates. Inmate Gatlin had some sort of article still in his pocket when Officer Burns reached him. Officer Burns forcibly shoved Inmate Gatlin against the wall and told him to stand there until he was ready for him. Inmate Gatlin then told Officer Burns that it was not necessary to shove him and Officer Burns became very angry. He again shoved Inmate Gatlin and struck him with his fist. A fight erupted and another inmate had to step between the officer and the inmate. Lt. Fred Watson, the Shift Supervisor, was called upon to investigate and he concluded that Officer Burns had apparently lost his temper. Lt. Watson advised Mr. Cecil Boren of the officer's actions and recommended that Officer Burns be terminated. Mr. Boren concurred in this opinion and Officer Burns was relieved of his duties immediately.

Sketch: "You didn't lose them goddamned shoes."

When they brought me back they brought me out there and I'm waiting outside the door and this colored boy lost his shoes. Well, I'm digging all the play, see. They had that tape recorder on and they had charged him with losing his shoes and he runs this story down that somebody had stole his shoes and he couldn't catch the line that morning. So they turned the tape recorder off and the man gets up in this colored boy's face and he said, "Now listen: you think you're gamin' with me. You didn't lose them goddamned shoes, you threw them shoes away. The next time you come out here and tell me you lost your shoes I'm gonna find some shoes and whip all the shit out of you with the shoes." Then they turned the tape recorder back on and said, "Now we're going to send you back to the building and don't you lose these shoes no more." I don't know if that's for the benefit of the court or what.

Tommy: "Inmate Smith, you have been found guilty . . ."

I'm gonna tell you about that disciplinary hearing now. They got that tape recorder. Now, let me tell you what they do. They punch that recorder and say, "Now, Inmate Smith, you are charged with rule violation three: fighting with or without a weapon. How do you plead to this charge?" That's for the record. Then you plead guilty or not guilty. Then they turn the motherfucker off and they say, "All right, you goddamned hardheaded motherfucker, you think you're running something around here, we're going to beat you half to death with these sticks and then you're going to think you're running something." They click it back on and say, "Now, Inmate Smith, you have been found guilty by the disciplinary committee and we're going to take so-and-so action" and all that shit.

6. Maximum Security

In their report of their design of the Maximum Security Unit, Little Rock architects Wittenberg, Delony, and Davidson give one a sense of a truly gorgeous facility:

The primary generator of the plan was the problem of separation and control of three different types of incarceration. The design solution was to group these modules around a central control center. Then the immediate physical needs of the inmate were defined and a basic unit was formulated. Noteworthy is how the solution goes beyond the problems of mechanical efficiency and into the creation of a meaningful environment completely free from cells or cell fronts.

From these criteria, a basic physical unit was determined for the structural and mechanical systems. Careful consideration was given, at this stage of development, to durability and economics of systems. Using this conceptual approach and a prime consideration to make the atmosphere of the areas as open as possible, the final product is a blend of beauty and operation efficiency in prison architecture.

The Department of Corrections Employee Handbook *reflects the optimism of the architects:*

The maximum security plant enables the staff to relieve much of the tension and pressure which inevitably results from housing maximum security inmates in minimum security barracks. Recalcitrant men are separated from the others.

Some inmates have a different vision of life in the white concrete structure.

Willie: "The guy had gone from a hundred fifty-five pounds to a hundred twenty-six pounds."

Out there in Maximum Security, they have inmates three and four to a cell. Last time I was out there I saw a inmate get raped out there. By force he had to perform two abnormal sexual acts. He was forced to commit what you call oral sex on another man, then he was forced to commit anal sex with another man. This isn't the first time that happened. A man filed a suit in federal court about the lack of security out there, how he was raped in isolation one time, but the wardens scared him and he pulled the lawsuit out.

Right now I have a hundred-and-eighty-thousand-dollar lawsuit in against the state. It consists of how the warden come out and whipped up the inmates and everything, how they made me walk across cut glass and I accumulated numerous cuts on the bottom of my foot, how they denied inmates in Maximum Security access to the federal courts by destroying their writs, and the outrageous commissary prices they set up here in the institution also.

The riot they had out there in the Maximum Security, where the inmates destroyed a whole bunch of property, that started because the superintendent promised the guys they would be able to eat on Christmas day. It's supposed to be a sacred day. Then he went back on his promise and the guys didn't feel he did them right. See, he said he was going to let them eat a tray of Christmas dinner and he didn't.

We don't eat but two pieces of bread and some grue [the

processed food for inmates in punitive isolation] out there. And actually, some don't eat but four slices of bread because this grue, they don't consume it in their body for the simple reason that it's not fitten to eat. This is just the men in Punitive.

So the guys didn't figure they were did right, so they started riotin', they tore up bowls, doorknobs, chairs off the walls and everything. Superintendent and them came out there and they jumped on the guys, jumped on a few of them, locked some of them up in a quiet cell.

One of the guys that was in that riot had been out in the hole five months, a little over five months. On two slices of bread and grue. Last time I was out there, which was a little over two weeks ago, the guy had gone from a hundred fifty-five pounds to a hundred twenty-six pounds.

The second riot started out there because in the hole every third day you receive a tray at twelve o'clock, a regular meal. And on this certain day we was supposed to get a tray and the warden brought us our tray back there, but it was such a small amount of food that the men knew that this warden was deliberately messing over them. And when it was brought to their attention the only thing they did was laugh. So the guys had no other alternative but to either accept that abuse or else go and show them how they actually felt about it.

So we chose to show them how we actually felt about it.

We threw our trays out in the hall, tore the doorknobs off the door, tore the table and bench that they have welded into the wall, we tore all this off, tore some of the commodes up also. Warden came out there, stepped on some of the guys, put some in the quiet cell, sprayed Mace all over everything, cussed 'em out. Wasn't nothing but black dudes in the riot anyway. Calling 'em "black motherfuckers" and "sonabitches." I was addressed as "nigger" one time by the major. That's what my lawsuit consists of, behind that incident.

I watch and every time I see a warden intimidate deliberately or misuse an inmate, I takes all this in, and the next writ I get ready to write, I put all this in. Not for my own benefit, but for all the inmates benefitin'.

I'm doin' nine years, but the Supreme Court reversed my conviction Thursday, so I'm goin' home sometime next week. But even though I'm going home Wednesday or Thursday I still intend to pursue all my allegations against the penitentiary once I'm on the outside.

Dirty Harry: ". . . Chinese Mulligan stew."

Grue looks like a hamburger. It's got maybe green beans, carrots, sweet potatoes, black-eyed peas. It's every damned thing you can name all mixed up into one. They bake it just like corn bread and cut it in slices. It gets hard.

It looks like some Chinese mulligan stew. And when you taste it, it tastes like shit.

Leslie: "I guess it's just death for me."

I'm in isolation at Cummins prison. I've been in isolation for sixty-three or sixty-four days and they're only supposed to keep you fifteen days without a doctor checking you and see if you're able to continue on this bread-and-water diet. And there's been no doctor checking me at all. I've lost down from a hundred thirty-five pounds to less than a hundred. They won't weigh me now. I don't know how much below a hundred I weigh. It's below a hundred.

The food that they feed you out here, the diet, I can't eat it. I have a bad stomach, I have only one lung, and I'm missing six ribs.

How did you lose your lung?

Got shot. Got shot with a shotgun. Got six ribs missing on that side and my shoulder blade. I'm not able to work. In order to get out of the hole I would have to agree to take this job and I can't do it because I just can't do it. So I guess I'm just here until I die.

You're expected to shave in here without mirrors. They bring you a razor around with a blade in it that's been shaved with maybe twenty or thirty times. They very seldom ever change them. And you're expected to shave without a mirror. I can't do this and don't intend to try. I know that I can't.

You can't get out of the hole unless you shave.

I have to take narcotics all this time. I've got to have it for my condition. They tell me that they run out of this medicine. I know that this is not true because one of the doctors that comes around has given me the medicine and then they tell me that they're out. I guess that's about it.

This man in the cell with me, the one who don't talk, he needs to be in a mental institution. I don't know what his name is. I certainly don't.

How did you get shot with the shotgun?

A fellow shot me about his wife. He thought I was fooling with his wife, which I wasn't, but he got the idea that I was and shot me point blank. He found out later that she just told him some lies. I never fooled with her. She was wanting to leave him to go to California with me and I wouldn't let her go and that was the reason that she told him that she'd been going out with me and I've never went out with the woman yet.

We got into a fight first and he went and got his shotgun and shot me. I got a damaged heart muscle. I'm supposed to be on a special diet. Hear of a high-protein diet? And they tell me here that they don't have such a diet. I dunno: I guess it's just death for me.

Have you filed any writs?

I filed several writs but I don't believe my mail is going out. Now, this ole lieutenant out here, there's two inmates told me that he throwed away some of my mail to the federal courts. I've got a package here, this food they feed you, and I send it to the federal courts daily. They give me that grue twice today and I've got letters from both St. Louis and Little Rock saying that they have received some of it, but I have a letter from Mr. Stiles saying that it's not wrapped properly and that he won't send it out no more and these two inmates tell me that the lieutenant throwed some in the trash and takes it to the incinerator and burns it up. I've got this thing from Stiles last night that he sent two packages back saying that it was not wrapped properly. I wrote the warden about this a number of times. He either don't care or he's scared to do anything about it.

Charles: "My teeth had got loose and my bones just ached. . . ."

An officer's always right.

I had a disciplinary last week. They put me in class four. They didn't put me in the hole but they found me guilty. Now I got to work another sixty days before I can even go up for class again. I was in class one. I been in class one since I got out of the hole.

What I got in the hole for. I'd come in from work because I got a bad sinus problem and my back was bothering me. When I got to the hospital, this is a situation when if you get sick out in the field and if you want to come in and the doctor say you're not sick, you're goin' to the hole. This is what it amounts to.

So I come in out of the field and went over there to the doctor. Dr. Ashley is over there, but Dr. Ashley didn't check me, he had another inmate check me. He took my temperature, my blood pressure, and my pulse. And evidently the inmate wrote it on a card and gave the card to the doctor. The doctor give me some medication, but he called the desk and told 'em wasn't nothing wrong with me.

When I went to the court, I explained to them that Dr. Ashley should have checked me himself because that amounted to another inmate sending me to the hole. You know how inmates do: they dislike each other, have little old idiosyncrasies and don't get along together. If he want to put me in the hole he can do that. I explained to him that the doctor should have checked me himself.

All this disciplinaries, whatever it is, it's always "disobey-ing a direct order" or "refusing to work." They don't put on there that the inmate was sick out in the field and come in and the doctor said he's not sick. I tried to explain to the doctor that all the sickness don't be in no temperature.

I stayed out there in the hole two months. But I just happened to be in the two little riots they had out there and they kept me out there. They hurt my side. That's part of the problem I got is with my side. I got a couple of lawsuits in now because of the injuries to my side. It hurts all the time.

Why had they jumped on you?

I had been out there fifty or sixty days and I had filed one lawsuit about my teeth. My teeth had got loose and my bones just ached, I just ached all over. I figured I wasn't getting enough vitamins and calories and so forth. I had to lay in my bed all the time, every time I got up I got dizzy, so I filed a lawsuit and tried to explain to the judge that my bein' in confinement like that per se it ain't cruel and un-usual, but after fifty or sixty days with no food and stuff your teeth start getting loose and your bones start hurting, you jaws start hurting, 'cause you don't get enough vi-tamins for your body.

And this is the biggest problem and I tried to explain it to him, to the judge, try to get him to do something to get me released from the hole.

After two months and six days they released me.

I ain't been having too many problems since then.

The cell out in punitive there is a one-man cell, but they have three persons in them, sometimes four. It's crowded.

You have to sleep where one's sleepin' at an angle, be stepping all over each other. It's got one bed in it 'way up off the floor. All day long you haven't got nothing to do, no benches to sit on, so all you can do is lay on the hard cold floor. See, only one inmate in there got the bed and he's laying on the bed. He's the one that got in there first. The other inmates just have to lay on the floor. And there's no lights in the cells or nothing. They expect you to shave with no mirror.

I haven't been out in the fields much, but I was in the hoe squads when I first come here. I think that was my main reason for going to isolation.

I tried to explain to them that I had just come in off the streets and they had me picking cotton, running. Hell, I never had picked any cotton before, and they have me running and working. Work nine hours a day. Go to work at seven in the morning work till five in the evening. You can't explain to them that you're not in condition to do this work. It may not be that hard, but a person that's not use to working, if he just stands up nine hours a day it's tiresome, can't hardly stand it.

7. The Death of Carl Vaughan

Despite the great changes that have taken place in the Arkansas prison system the past five or six years, potential for grievous abuse still exists. A prison is like any other bureaucracy: its first order of business, before all others, is self-preservation; decisions are made at all levels with a constant pressure to avoid heat, avoid problems, avoid outside attention, avoid disruption. Events or persons that challenge the order of the institution are seen as serious threats.

Refusal to work threatens the economic and ideological bases of southern prison systems. Inmate strikes have been dealt with violently in the past: guards would rush in with hoses and clubs and shotguns and they would break bones until the strikers agreed to go back to the fields. Guards can't do that any more, so they revert to more subtle forms of harassment. Offending inmates are transferred so they won't continue to instigate trouble (after the 1971 Attica rebellion, all the inmates identified as having taken part in the events in D Yard were scattered among other New York institutions), and they are often given a hard time at their new locations.

But sometimes it goes too far. It killed Carl Vaughan. He was moved, harassed, beaten by inmates with guard sanction. He got little sleep and little food. And he died.

No one wanted Carl Vaughan to die. Some people wanted him to suffer a lot, but not to die. His death caused all kinds of problems, it even brought in a state police investigation. He died, one prison board member told·me, because no one cared enough to make sure he didn't, because no one cared enough for him as a human being.

His death is anomalous, freaky, but the lack of simple human care isn't. It is a factor in all institutional life—in colleges and hospitals as well as prisons—but it matters more in prison because there is so little else.

Gus: "He said, 'I think they're gonna kill me.' "

It was August twenty-second. A boy named Carl Vaughan was sent to this Cummins unit from Tucker. Tucker is the intermediate reformatory for offenders under twenty-one, first offenders. Carl was twenty-one years old, white, and he was accompanied by ten other inmates. The reason they were being sent to Cummins was for disciplinary purposes. This has been denied by the Department of Corrections. The Department of Corrections states that these same men were transferred here at their own request. The only discrepancy about this statement is that they failed to mention that the transfer committee at Tucker is exactly the same as the disciplinary committee at Tucker. The same people preside on both committees.

According to the statements that we received from five inmates, all said that they were asked immediately before the punishment was assessed whether they had any objection to going to Cummins, and this, of course, was at a time when they were waiting for their good time to be taken away and their class four [which earns no good time] awarded to them, which would mean a loss of good time for x number of months. They knew that if they answered no, we want to stay at Tucker, they may never get their good time back and they may remain a class four forever, so each one of them said, "No, we have no objections," because this is the disciplinary committee that's talking to them.

Immediately after these boys were dismissed from the disciplinary committee, the transfer committee met and took action and effected the transfer for all eleven of them.

These boys, incidentally, appeared before the disciplinary committee because of the nature of their offense, which was that they had refused to go to work. The reason they refused to go to work was because they had maintained that they had been fed pink pork or at least defective pork which made them sick, gave them diarrhea and cramps. They insisted on being taken to the hospital for a medical examination and they were taken to the hospital and given a very cursory examination by the attending doctor. He felt their foreheads and their stomachs and told them to go to work. When they refused—saying that their cramps wouldn't allow them to go to work—they were placed in the hole. They stayed in the hole, maximum security, at Tucker, for thirteen days, and at the end of thirteen days they were transferred to punitive isolation cells and fed a restricted diet for three days. This was immediately prior to their transfer to Cummins, so now we're back to August the twenty-second.

They were transferred to Cummins and arrived here at five-thirty in the morning. They were immediately sent to the building major's office, the major in charge of all custody for the Cummins unit, and were browbeaten and threatened into almost total submission. After they left the major's office, they were sent out the sally-port gate to await the work call.

When they were being loaded onto the trailers, Carl Vaughan was singled out for reasons that no one really knows as the scapegoat and to be the example for the whole group. It was obvious from the beginning that they were there to be punished. Carl, for example, was shifted from one trailer to another by the officer. When he finally settled down onto the trailer that he was assigned to, the sign was passed—some sort of signal from the correctional officer to the inmate on board the wagon—to harass this Carl Vaughan. Carl was kicked and thrown back from group to group in the trailer and completely frightened and intimidated. By the time he got to work in the field, one of the statements from one of the inmates revealed that he was shaking so hard and was so frightened that he could scarcely work. He went to the water wagon to get a drink of water on several occasions during the morning and each time he was forced to the rear of the line, with the result that he would get very little, if any, water at all at the water call. He was repeatedly hit with mud clods, kicked, knocked down, and at one point lost his shoes in the mud in the ditch that he was digging in. The officer in charge refused to allow him to get his shoes. He was forced to work barefoot for the remainder of the morning, some hour and a half.

Inmates were hitting them, but at the direction and with the full acquiescence of the guards. One statement says, "What was the officer doing all this time?" and the guy said, "Well, the officer would look and see him, Vaughan, being beaten and he would turn his head and he'd wait about three or four minutes and then he'd turn back and he'd say, 'You all better stop that now.' But he'd be sure to wait three or four minutes."

Vaughan came in to lunch with no particularly startling events happening at lunch, but when he returned to the field in the afternoon, about two o'clock, he told another inmate, "Gordon, I don't think I can make it. I feel like I'm gonna pass out. I just can't make it." Gordon told him to try to hang on. He said, "I think they're gonna kill me."

About four o'clock, five minutes to four in the afternoon, on August the twenty-second, Carl Vaughan passed out completely and couldn't be revived. Water was thrown in his face three times and with no effect. He was then dragged, literally dragged by the heels, up to the wagon and thrown on the wagon. The wagon proceeded toward the main buildings.

When it had gone about three or four hundred yards, somebody on the trailer yelled, "I think he's dead." And with that, the trailer was stopped. The body was taken off the trailer, loaded on a pickup truck, and rushed to the unit infirmary.

The man in attendance at the unit infirmary stated that in his opinion Carl Vaughan was dead on arrival, that when he tried to give artificial resuscitation the lips were cold, that the hands were already starting to show the results of rigor mortis, that the eyes were open and staring, that the lids wouldn't close. This same paramedic stated that in his opinion—although he is not particularly skilled in viewing dead bodies—in his particular opinion, that this boy had

been mistreated, that he was a mass of filth from head to toe, that he showed signs of beating around the face, that he had dried blood around the corners of his mouth, dried blood at the nose, and had a peculiar lump on the back of his head, and that one of his hands was scarred and skinned recently.

As a result of all this, by the time the inmates and the unit found out what had happened, the excitement or the antagonism was running pretty high. Several of us took statements from five of the inmates that were actually involved, five that were willing to give us statements, which detailed pretty much the story that I've told you.

In retaliation, the state, or the administration, called in these five inmates after a very cursory investigation by the CID, which was designed primarily to intimidate these same five. After this investigation, the administration told these men that they either must sign a repudiation of their original statements, saying that they had been forced or coerced into giving a statement, and be rewarded by being returned to Tucker, or, if they refused to repudiate their statements, they would be sent to Seven Barracks and would be killed.

Two of the inmates—Gordon Merrill and Earl Hungerford—refused to sign the administration's waver and they were placed in Maximum Security, where they are to this day. Both reside in cells out at Maximum Security. No disciplinary action has ever been taken against either of these boys, but they nevertheless refused to repudiate what they know to be true.

In the meantime, the other inmates that recanted their

statements were returned to Tucker. There have been investigations launched and aborted and two lawyers have been appointed by the judge to represent Merrill and Hungerford in their 1984 actions. This is an action for injunctive relief that's brought into federal court. They have taken statements from both these inmates and I understand have initiated action in the Pine Bluff division of the federal district court. Gordon Merrill, to my understanding, has already been in court as of last Friday and has entered some testimony, probably similar to the rendition I'm giving now. Both have sued for seventy-five thousand dollars.

Prison Commissioner T. D. Hutto: ". . . the credibility of the abuse allegations are highly suspect."

The investigation report on the death of Carl Joe Vaughan, an inmate at Cummins State Prison Farm, was given to the press yesterday by Arkansas prison officials, but no major new information was included.

Both guards and inmate coworkers agreed that Vaughan became involved in several scuffles with other inmates August 22, the day he died.

Vaughan, 21, was serving 15 years from Washington County for armed robbery. He entered prison in November, 1974.

The investigation report included interviews with 22 other inmates, Cummins officials, medical workers, an autopsy report from the office of the state medical examiner, and an account of reports to the federal courts in reply to inmate allegations of brutality to Vaughan before his death.

The earlier official accounts of Vaughan's death stood unchanged, although there was much detail that had previously been withheld.

According to the state medical examiner, Vaughan died from heatstroke, although he had a black eye and a few other bruises on his body.

Terrell Don Hutto, state Correction commissioner, was asked why a healthy man of 21 had died, if there were no factors such as a beating involved in his death, and whether the Correction Department was responsible.

Hutto replied, "Until medical authorities answer for us why the body cooling mechanism goes haywire, I don't see that we can be found responsible."

. . . Hutto also was unable to say whether or not the punishment meals, an unappetizing all-in-one meat and vegetable cake, known as grue, contained significant amounts of salt.

Vaughan was fed meals of grue while confined on punishment status at Tucker Intermediate Reformatory for three days prior to his 5 a.m. transfer to Cummins on August 22.

Prison officials earlier conceded that through an "oversight," Vaughan and 10 others transferred between units that morning were not given breakfast. . . .

[Hutto] declined to fix blame for the oversight upon any official, saying that "a number of people" were responsible.

The transfer's early hour was because the same vehicle was needed later in the day to bring in new inmates from jails around the state, according to a report by Hutto.

Hutto said the officers in charge of Vaughan that day, Bennie Collins and his supervisor, David Reed, acted to take the inmate to the infirmary when he collapsed on the trailer as the crew was taken in from work. No first aid was administered in the field or on the truck, Hutto said, because it was preferred to have professionals treat him at the Cummins infirmary.

No disciplinary action had been taken against any officer, Hutto said, and none was expected.

He rejected inmate allegations that the two (Collins and Reed) beat Vaughan the day of his death. [Marshall N. Rush, chairman of the state correction board], in his statement, said that of 22 inmate accounts, 15 reported no beatings, while only seven alleged brutality.

Hutto's report said, "the credibility of the abuse allegations are highly suspect." Reed and Collins have years of experience and good records with the department, he said.

Hutto also said that both had received in-service training on recognizing heatstroke from Larry Hundley, the registered nurse at the Cummins infirmary. [*Pine Bluff Commercial,* November 1, 1975]

"Field supervisors did not apply first aid to Vaughan. . . ."

The state Correction Board yesterday adopted a detailed policy governing work by inmates in hot weather and providing for control of possible heat stroke by frequent ingestion of water and salt.

The policy was a reaction to the death of an inmate last August at Cummins State Prison Farm. Carl Joe Vaughan, 21, died of heat stroke after a day at work in the fields, according to an autopsy report by the office of the state medical examiner.

There was a State Police investigation of the incident that resulted in no legal action by the prosecuting attorney, and correction officials upheld officers supervising Vaughan, saying they found no fault with the care given the inmate.

Prison officials conceded that one error from one prison unit to another [*sic*], in that no breakfast was given to Vaughan that day. They had said that was not associated with Vaughan's death.

The seven-page statement of policy approved by the board calls for documented first-aid training for all employees who supervise inmates in the field of recognizing and treating heat injuries.

Kitchen employees are ordered to see that hot weather meals include ample salt, to help keep field workers in good health. . . .

For new inmates, the policy calls for a period of acclimatization to field work in hot-weather conditions extending over a two-week period.

The policy calls for first-aid remedies in the field for those suffering ill-effects from the heat, including removal of clothing, applications of water and rubbing of the skin to increase circulation.

Field supervisors did not apply any first aid to Vaughan, according to correction officials, because it was deemed best to wait for professional medical care at the infirmary.

In other business yesterday, the board approved working drawings for construction of a $490,000 administration building at Pine Bluff. . . . [*Pine Bluff Commercial,* March 21, 1976]

Farrel Gene Knight: "Entire Mentality"

Miller Williams, the well-known American poet, was for a while commuting to Cummins once or twice a month from his home four hundred miles away. He was giving poetry classes to small groups at the men's and women's units at Cummins (the women's unit has since moved up to Pine Bluff). When I met him, Williams was making the trips at his own expense because no Arkansas agency was interested in funding an activity as frivolous as poetry instruction. "But I think it's important," Williams said, "and some of those people, they really need it."

Williams was just about to leave for his home. We talked awhile about the prison, agreed to exchange books, said good-bye. Then I went over to the building to start working again.

A surprising thing happened: several very hard convicts, one of whom has never been without a pistol (save for prison time) or a knife since puberty, told me it was too bad I hadn't arrived a day earlier. "There was a real heavy dude here," one said, "someone you ought to know." The "real heavy dude" was Williams. For convicts like that to describe a thin, bearded free-world poet in such terms was a rare compliment.

Miller was right: the work he was doing was important and it was something some of those men needed desperately. He gave them a voice. There is a lot one would like to say in prison but cannot because there is no one to say such things to: you can't describe the anguish of the wasted years because everyone around you has the same anguish; you can't describe the oppression of the bars and wire and guns because everyone around you suffers the same oppression; you can't proclaim outrage because everyone has his own.

But a poem is a letter to the world, and in it you may say whatever you think needs saying. The poetry workshops started by Miller Williams at Cummins gave voice and a forum to men without either. Some of the poems reminded me of the black convict worksongs that existed for so many years in southern prisons: in those songs, men would sing of things they couldn't ever say, because the poetry of the songs allowed more things to be uttered than the prose of conversation ever could.

What follows is a poem by a convict who was in Williams' workshop. It was written after Williams left Arkansas and had gone on a fellowship to Rome. It arrived in the mail, handwritten on a long sheet of lined paper, as I was finishing the manuscript part of this book. It is Farrel Gene Knight's letter to the world.

It can't be, but it's happening to me!
I know this is it . . . the real thing.

The sweat in my eyes is killing my ass
Or is this "convict" doing the job?

The Man thinks it's all a joke,
This kind of shit is his main stroke.
"Kick those punks' ass, and make it good.
Do this up right, "Boy," we'll make you class one."
And the sun just keeps getting hotter.

There's dirt in my mouth Mother, and
Hate in my heart, And all the good people
Out there wonder why.
I don't know if I can handle much more,
And I'm too proud to break down and cry.
These ain't tears in my eyes you see,
Just the sweat that's running out of me.

Man, I'm trying' cause I know I'm dyin'.
If I can just make today, one more day
That's all I need, one day Lord. . . . Please!

But that ain't good enough, 'cause "Bootmouth"
Has to get his kicks, and Captain Carr wants his licks. ·
Oh, what the hell, it's all going to be over in a little while,
And in the years ahead, I'll look back and smile.

The blood, the dirt, sun, all of it is so real.
And the most real of it all . . . DEATH!

I can't go on with this 'cause that dude
Couldn't go on out there in them fields. He gave it
Up, and I'm givin' it up, but let me ask you this:

Is it Cummins Brutality?
No! says the doctor.
No! No! says the Man.
No! says the Court.
No! Fuck no.

Don't sweat it Carl Vaughan . . . it's just the
Entire Mentality.

Carl Vaughan died in August of 1975 from "Exhaustion,"
so it was ruled. But we all know here that he was beaten to
death by inmates! And Capt. Carr (among others) . . . administration. Capt. Carr has been fired and the whole incident has been swept under the rug. Oh, and by the way,
Carl Vaughan was sent home and stuck in the dirt.

And so it goes!

8. It Was a Brutal Way

Sketch: ". . . try to get even for the years . . . wasted right here."

I was twenty-five years old. I fell out of Little Rock. My first offense. I took three shirts out of a department store. They charged me with grand larceny. I don't know if I should have been charged with shoplifting or grand larceny, but the shirts were valued at fifty-three dollars.

Is fifty dollars the grand larceny cutoff?

Fifty dollars was the minimum and my charge was fifty-three, so they charged me with grand larceny. The judge sentenced me to fifteen years down here. The first day that I was here—I had no medical examination at all—they run me to the field and hit me fifteen times with that strap in the crack of my ass for just coming here. I had committed no prison rule violations whatsoever.

I stayed in that longline for two calendar years, then I got me a job as a baker in the bakery and I worked there, then I got a job in the canteen. I stayed here nine calendar years and six months and they discharged me. When I got out of here, I was full of hate to think that a state judge would sentence me—twenty-five years old, a first felony conviction. In the meantime I had met safecrackers, robbers and everything. And I felt like society owed me something.

And when I got out of here, that was my first thing: to try to get even for the years that I'd wasted right here. All right. I stayed out eighteen months. And during this time I'm steady stealing, steady cracking safes. In the meantime I'd done progressed to a safecracker, started using narcotics.

I got a bust. And this same judge that sentenced me to the fifteen strapped a twenty-one on me. This was in 1967. That was for four counts of burglary and three counts of burglary tools. So I came back in 1967. I stayed here three months. They put me on my same job—commissary.

I stayed here the three months and I run off. I was apprehended in Oklahoma and they filled after-former-conviction on me just because I had that one previous conviction they knew about and gave me twelve years. So I flattened that time in Oklahoma. I did six years in Oklahoma. That was two-for-one. I finagled around and spent four or five hundred dollars buying good time and I got out about six or eight months early.

The Oklahoma riot come down in July of 1973 and after the riot took place they started kicking people loose because they didn't have any accommodations for them. They sent me to the work release. Arkansas had neglected to put a detainer on me for that escape charge, so Oklahoma released me.

After I got out of Oklahoma there was nothing for me to do but start stealing again. I stayed out two weeks. The first job I went on was a rehash of a clinic I had made back in the fifties, and it went so good I went back to it for a rehash. I made the score, but the next day they busted us in a motel.

Somebody snitch you out?

Yeah. We stayed at this motel too long and the motel man got suspicious of us. The bust come down that night. So they gave me another twenty-one, running with my old one that I had. So I got two twenty-ones running concurrent now. They didn't file the bitch [charge him as a habitual criminal] on me. That was part of the plea bargaining: that I'd cop to the maximum and they'd run it together.

They put me in class four. You don't earn no good time, you do day for day. I've been up before that classification board four times since I've been back. They said, "We've got nothing for you."

This rule violation [i.e., his escape] was committed eight years ago. These people wasn't even here, different people was running the penitentiary then. The rule violation didn't exist then because there was no rulebook here then. They call it "leaving the assigned area." But they didn't even have a rulebook when I run off. All they had was a four-foot piece of hide and that was your punishment. Now this rulebook come into effect four years after I left. Four years after I left they print this rulebook and I'm hit with a violation that wasn't even in existence then.

Last year they had an attempted escape out at the laundry. Two guys getting out. They put a dummy in their cell. Both of 'em are loaded with time—one's doing thirty and the other's doing twenty. They're loaded, they got no out. So they put a dummy and one of these rats snitched on 'em about the dummy. So in the meantime, they go to the laundry, they're hid out there. When they go to the laundry, they kick all the shit out of them. And I'm a witness on that. They got it in federal court. But the federal court's not doing anything. It's been filed six months now and the federal court's not doing anything.

Here's what I'm trying to tell you: that the conditions in the Oklahoma penitentiary at the time they burnt twenty million dollars' worth of property are far less worse than the conditions here. In every respect: clothing, food, housing and everything. Now the convicts in Oklahoma, they had their own cells, they could do everything. They had more privileges as far as living conditions . . . There's no yard privileges here, you never get to go outside except to work.

The only reason why this penitentiary isn't being burnt and tore down today is for the simple reason that your general population here is nothing but cotton-patch niggers and white farmers. When they start getting the militant group out of the cities, they'll tear this sonofabitch down.

They're working fourteen, sixteen hours a day in these old muddy clothes around here, they drag up and down these halls and work their ass off. Myself, I don't feel sorry for them. Because if they're weak enough to go for it, more power to them. But they're not going to mistreat me like that. 'Cause I'll lay in that hole. I did a year of solitary confinement. One calendar year inside one of them cells.

Out of the last twenty years, I've been free sixteen months.

Tommy: "They don't want you to have nothing."

The day I come in, they strip me off naked, they took everything I had, man. They said my heels on my shoes was too big, they just stole them motherfuckers. They stole my jewelry I had on me. I had a chain, you know. They take that and say I can get it back when I get through doing this twenty-five-year-sentence. I know I ain't gonna get that

IT WAS A BRUTAL WAY

shit back. They strip me naked and tell me they going to kill me right off the bat. Tell me, "You think you're going to run."

I said, "Look, I been doing time a long time now. I ain't never had a prison escape or attempted escape."

He said, "You ain't never had twenty-five years before, have you?"

I said, "No, you're right there."

He said, "I'm gonna tell you what: you run off, you harm one of these officers or something, I'm gonna kill you, that's all there is to it. I'm gonna kill your fucken ass."

And if you rair up, they say, "Well, this old thing's got fight in him. What are we going to do with this old thing? He's got fight in him."

They're really country down here, man.

They don't want you to have nothing. They want you to lay on that bunk twenty-four hours a day if you're not working or assigned. They want you laying on that bunk looking at that ceiling. If you're working, they want you to run out there and work your fucken ass off, come back in here and lay on your bunk till you go to work the next morning.

Cooter: "You was gonna take that shotgun if that man wanted you to."

If you let one get away on you, you might as well go with him.

Plus getting all the hell whipped out of you, you wouldn't get a parole, you'd flatten your time and you'd do it in the longline.

What would happen when a convict guard got thrown back in the ranks?

He didn't have too good a future. He just had a long row and a wide one to hoe. It got pretty tough.

You look at it this way: you've turned against your own man. You're doing time like he is. He's got as much right to guard you as you've got to guard him. The good guys stay in the whites [line inmate uniforms are white], and them old sorry trusties take them shotguns and high-powers.

But you did get a reward for it in a way. You got to eat better, you had better clothes, you had more privileges, you had green money, you could wear any kind of clothes you want, you could visit without anybody sitting there and listening to everything you said, and some of 'em got furloughs. And there was a good chance of you getting out when you went up for parole if you took that shotgun.

You was gonna take that shotgun if that man wanted you to. If that bullhide lasted and you lasted, you was gonna take that shotgun. If you stop and think about it, why not go ahead and take it instead of going through all that punishment? 'Cause he's gonna have his guards. You was gonna do what he said to do.

And if you let a man get away from you, that's when you went back in there with all them fellas that you done kept there.

It mostly depended on the warden. I did most of my time over at Tucker, but it was the same rules.

They had escape hide. It was different from the regular

bullhide. It was thicker, a little bit longer, and some of 'em had hacksaw blades in 'em in the end.

Some used to have—I didn't see this—four silver dollars sewed in the end of them. But just the regular bullhide was enough to get anything they wanted out of you. I got that five times. It hurt pretty bad, but it didn't do me no physical harm. It just made me mad, plenty of that.

I just rather take my chances with that rank man and not have to take that bullhide. You can hold a gun on a man and still treat him right. You don't have to take that shotgun and shoot him, you don't have to take that rifle and shoot him. A man's a man, it don't make any difference if he's rank man or trusty or what he is.

Now there's still some trusties. We sleep together over there. The ones in that tower, they got guns on us. And they come right in there at night and lay down and go to sleep. And they will shoot you. If a man don't believe it, all he's gotta do is go over there and climb up over that fence and see. I'm pretty sure they're not going to go get a warden to handle the gun and have him do it, because he's gonna be putting some soil between here and there by that time.

What did the free man do in the old days?

He just whupped ass.

And the convict ran the place?

The convict trusty in those days was more than a warden [free-world guard] is now. They had the power and they had the administration behind them. That was the onliest way the penitentiary could function was with the trusties.

You had some trusties here that didn't deserve to carry a gun in his hand. You had some of 'em that got out of here and got killed just for the fact that he had carried a gun in here.

They don't no trusty leave this penitentiary and go to another joint but what there is somebody in that joint either had been here and knew him or else when his record comes from this penitentiary to the one he went to, it had "Good for information" wrote on it. And if it had that, he was a trusty. And if you cooperated with the warden, it had that on it: "Cooperative with warden" meant that you would give them information—which is a snitch—and you was a trusty.

If I had a choice, I'd say, put the penitentiary back the way it was fifteen years ago. Let a man know where he stands at, what to expect, and that way you can cope with it. An old inmate can't get used to this.

Wasn't it a lot more violent and dangerous and brutal then?

It was. There was reasons for a lot of that. But you could do time then, you could do time.

But now they have that pencil. You take one of these pencils here and mess a man up for twenty years if he got twenty years. If you get three minor disciplinaries and that'll mount up to a major. Well, you could take that bullhide and whenever you got up and got through rubbin' it, it was over with, that was all of it. They didn't put those whuppin's on them jackets [they didn't record the offenses in an inmate's official file]. They put the whuppin's on the seat of your britches and that's where it stopped at. But a disciplinary goes in that jacket, it stays in there and goes to the parole board with you and they go over that.

So that's the reason I say put it back like it was.

They were pretty free with the hide in those days.

That's the one thing they weren't short of. They'd get short of groceries, they got short of men, but didn't get short of no whippin'. Warden may get tired, I seen that happen.

The riders had a rubber hose with a spark plug in the end of it. They'd do head-whupping. I seen one get shot on account of it—Hobart Williams. I wrote about him on that paper I gave you last year.

The warden on the longline, that was in '58, he was whuppin' him. I'd just got up from it myself. I'd got behind cuttin' corn stalks eatin' a bar of candy. I went down and got my little helping of it and Hobart was behind me. They hit him about one lick. He got up and was running down the turn row and Bob Lee Watson shot him right under the rib cage with a, I believe it's a .351. And he just melted right there.

They didn't whip him no more.

It was a brutal way. You just didn't know if you was going to come in at night when you went out there. Wasn't any way you could know. But to me it was a better way. These short hairs, I don't know if they understand that.

Is there any way you think it has changed for the good since the old days here?

I don't think I can say that and be honest with myself.

The biggest letdown an inmate's got here is one of them little old handbooks. It'll tell you what to do to try to shorten your time. It's signed by Mr. Hutto. You go out there and go by every rule they got here and you know then they haven't got no reason for denying you by the parole board and they're supposed to give you thirty days a month for wearing these khakis plus the thirty you do [trusties get two-for-one good time, credit for two days for each day actually served]. You go up there and they got no reason to deny you on your past record and yet they give you a year's denial. What feeling would you have?

It didn't do me no good in the world to wear these khakis and keep my business straight. But I'm gonna keep straight anyway unless somebody gets it wrong.

What good does that good time do me? It only does good if you flatten out or if you make parole the first time up, which is maybe ten out of every thirty. The rest of the boys that makes parole has already been up there and got a year's denial or six months, so actually the parole board is holding this population here.

They're not going to ever give somebody that's been in twice before, like you, parole in the first time around, are they?

Very seldom. It happens, but very seldom. You can't predict that parole board.

The trouble with this parole board is, they carry a man up there and the first thing they ask him is "How many times you been here?"

Well, now, you done paid for all that. If you gotta go back

through court every time you try to get out of here, then nobody who goes up there without a lawyer is gonna make it.

If you got to buy a parole, how can parole be a privilege? Anything you buy is not a privilege. There's people in here that can't even buy tobacco. How could they afford a lawyer?

And half the board members is lawyers. If you got a lawyer to go up there with you, when they start bringing that past record up on you, well, he tells them right there, "Let's hold up there. The charge is the one the man is in here on now."

They couldn't even show a disciplinary on me. My record was as blank as that seat is there. All they had in there was my commitment, no disciplinary. But they denied me because I'd been in here before. Seriousness of the nature of the crime. But the court tried me because of that.

Before, you could kind of go, you was expecting it, you wasn't promised nothing. You knew you was gonna do a third of that time when you come in that gate out there. You wasn't expecting to go out before that. If you was a first-time loser, you had that parole. If you had a year when you come here, you stayed four months out of that year and you was going to get that parole unless you run off. You wouldn't get it then. But you come in here now doing a year, you come in getting ready to go back out. You go up and they say you haven't done enough time. But if you don't have enough time, how come they put you up before the board?

Sketch: "They spray you like you're a fucken goat. . . ."

When you first hit this place, they line you up out there in the hall and you go in and there's the big major sitting there.

They strip you and they spray you. They spray you like you're a fucken goat or something.

There's a little game that they play. When you first get here, they try to give you the impression, "I'm Mr. Toughguy, you ain't nothing." They'll get right up in your face and say, "Hey, you one of them smart sonofabitches that tried to beat that jail up there? Whyn't you try to beat me?" They provoke you.

I really don't see why these guys don't get together. Course, like I say, you just haven't got the type of people here that you've got in Oklahoma. Even though they're abusing them every day, they just let 'em get by.

I used to eat soybeans in the field with no meat. The only time you got meat back here in the fifties and sixties was you got one piece of rabbit and that was on Sunday. So help me God, and I can verify it, and I was here for nine calendar years, I never seen more than one piece of rabbit in that mess hall. You got no beef or pork or anything. You ate soybeans, you ate turnip greens and onion tops. They had what they call a onion top soup here. They take onion tops and break 'em up and add water to it and salt and serve that.

They've started feeding now, they've started feeding.

But in a way, I would rather do time under the old system even though they was starving 'em and beating 'em to death down here. I would rather do time under the old system than I had under this system here for the simple reason that these guards, they'll humiliate you, they'll provoke you. You can't even have a piece of cardboard to write a letter, they'll confiscate it. You can't even have a light.

Under the old system, you knew where you stood. If you committed some kind of violation, that hide hurts. And they misused it. They'd hit you up here, they used to. But you take somebody that'll use the hide, he'll hit you five or six times and you're on your way. To me, that's better punishment than sitting me in a straight-back chair and telling me to shell a gallon of peanuts. Shit.

How long does it take to get a gallon?

A long time. Sometimes two or three days, man. I'm serious! You think you'll go out there and fill that can, that a gallon of peanuts ain't nothing. Shit: you be dreaming about peanuts.

Bird: ". . . This inmate has been made a slave of."

Here in the prison, there are four known classes of inmate statuses. Class one, class two, class three, and class four. A class one inmate receives thirty days a month extra good time. Class two receives twenty days allotted extra good time a month. Class three receives eight. Class four receives none.

In the United States constitutional law, it is said that a prison and an armed services personnel can be forced to work, but isn't it right for them to be compensated for their work? To work a man and not pay him is making a slave out of that man. To force him to work and not paying him is making a slave out of that man. Class four inmates do not receive any measure of good time at all, and nobody gets any money. Therefore this inmate has been made a slave of.

Kid: "If I had two hundred dollars I'd put it in that man's hand. . . ."

I found a 1916 dime when I was pulling cotton. Picked it up, rubbed the clay off, saw it was 1916, and kept going. Got to the end of the row—I'd only been out there for a few days—I said, "I found a 1916 dime, sir." You know, away from the other guys.

He said, "Let me see it." I gave it to him. He say, "What'll you take for it?"

I said, "Nothing." I had been thinking less than five minutes before I hit that spot, "If I had two hundred dollars I'd put it in that man's hand just to take it easy on me while I'm out here and let me get out of here without any disciplinaries." I put that in his hand and I went away and we're great. He got me out of the hoe squad in forty-eight days when we're supposed to spend sixty out there. He gave me the easy jobs, like gouging.

Gouging, or striking, but it's popularly known as gouging, if we were picking cucumbers, there would be one or two guys on a row. They're bent over all day. Terrific. Filling their sacks. The sack man comes behind with the empty sacks and he dumps it all in there. Then he goes and gets cucumbers from the other guys and takes them off the row. You're standing up all day. You have to carry a heavier sack because you're carrying all the other men's cucumbers, but you're standing. And gouging when they're hoeing is when they're carrying a row hoeing and you're going behind them catching what they miss. Which gets difficult at times if two guys are 'way behind and your bossman wants them to catch up. You have to work twice as hard helping those guys catch up.

Myles: "I don't think prison authorities want the inmates to use the law library."

I think the biggest problem around here is use of the law library. I don't think prison authorities want the inmates to use the law library. You know, Judge Henley, three or four years ago, he declared this institution unconstitutional, and it still is. We get to use the law library every other night. But can't two persons out of each barracks go to the law library at the same time. So you might get to use the law library once every two weeks or three weeks.

The law library stays open for two hours, but you don't be in the law library. You can check books out and take them into the mess hall. So you can't use 'em sometimes because another inmate be using 'em. It's insufficient anyway, they need a lot of books they haven't got.

Like an inmate, if he don't know nothing about law, he go down there and the clerk in the law library, if he ask for a book, he don't know what to give him. And a person may go down there not knowin' nothing about law, it may take him two or three months to find the book he wants. Where if he could go in a library and look around and look through books while he in there, he may be able to find something sort of what he's lookin' for.

I got two rap partners and both of 'em is in the hole now for tryin' to use the law library. One of them, he went down to the law library the other night. They told him there was already two people at the law library out of six barracks, so he tells the warden that he want to go down and talk to the lieutenant. Well, he went down and talked to the lieutenant, and the lieutenant told him that he couldn't use the law library, that he could put restrictions on it because of security reasons. My rap partner explained to him that two and three hundred people go to the movie and nobody says nothing, and five and six hundred go down there and eat at the same time and there ain't no security risk, but can't but six or eight people go down and use the law library. He got in an argument and after it all turned out, there wasn't nobody in the law library at all anyway.

Assistant Superintendent Michaels: "It was very unorganized when I first came up here."

In comparison to what was here—all I know is from '71, the latter part of '71—the major changes have been made from the standpoints of just actually cleaning the physical plant itself up. Being able to give an inmate clothes, proper wearing apparel, the living facilities themselves, even though they are still overcrowded to some extent, not as much as they were, being able to give proper bedding to the inmates. I think the biggest change that has been made since '71 is just the actual living conditions for the inmate himself. In this, too, is the fact that we have been able to acquire more employee help, more correctional officers, more positions for correctional officers. Although we still haven't got as many as we would like to have, we're still a heck of a lot better than we were in 1971 when I first came here.

That and just pure control of the inmate by organization of the institution. It was very unorganized when I first came up here. There were no set patterns to follow, no outline, it was just do as you can when you can.

There was no educational program when I first came here and now we have—though it's in its first year, its first six months—what I think is a pretty darned good educational system. I think we've worked on our vocational program to the point where we're trying to put in the program the kind of inmate that it will benefit. Put a guy in that we're pretty sure will get out shortly after he finishes the training, which I've advocated. There's not much sense putting a guy in who's doing ten years, putting a guy into a vocational program shortly after he comes into the institution. Then there's maybe nine years and six months before he goes out and uses this vocation, you know?

We're in the process of adding some industry. Even though it's small, even though Arkansas is primarily an agricultural state, agriculture has its industries, so therefore I think a lot of these guys will be going out and working in industry and just being able to work in the industry here and getting used to the cycle or process—I guess you might say production—getting used to it would help some.

Things like duplication, clothing manufacture in the women's reformatory, records conversion. These are small, but you got to walk before you can run. I feel like we'll have more industry later.

We have a lot of construction going on for a small system. The last construction that was done here, an outside construction company came in and did the job. A couple of inmates helped, but that was about all. And now the inmates are doing all the work on the construction. Some of these guys come off the streets with a construction occupation and they can go on with it while they're in the institution. As time goes on, processes change and we try to keep up with as modern an operation as they do outside. So guys won't lose out when they go back out to work on construction, and some of the guys working on construction will have in fact a new occupation when they walk out. They'll have a new trade, if they want to use it.

Of course it all comes down to dollars and cents. We save the state, the taxpayers, a lot of money by doing it ourselves, we know that. But you do keep the inmates busy and I believe in that—keeping them occupied as many hours of the day as you possibly can, whether it be at work, recreation, or school, whathaveyou, to keep his mind occupied, 'cause I have the feeling that those hours when you're idle are hard time.

I don't know. I guess don't anybody know that hasn't been there.

Lester: "You just close your eyes. . . ."

You see we got paper cups now. That's an improvement. When you first came down here they came around with that bucket and there'd be just a few cups and everybody'd use those same cups. We use the cups and then those punks, those cocksuckers, used the same cups. The first time you get a water break you try to see what cup they used, but the second time they're all mixed up together, so you just close your eyes, pick one, and hope.

George: "It's easier to make it here now."

I think this place has changed for the better. It's easier to make it here now. Those guys who told you it's changed for the worse, they're long-termers. The one I heard talking to you yesterday, he had a good job before, in the old head-busting days. Maybe the others were guards or something like that. They had better food and living conditions than everybody else. They got to go into town. They got furloughs. Now they're treated like any other convict and they don't like that.

9. The Cummins Carol

"You like poetry?" someone asked me in the cotton patch near the water wagon one October afternoon. I said I did. "You come by Eight Barracks tonight," the man said, "and I'll give you a poem about this place." I went up to the building that night and this is what the man gave me:

Twas the night after Christmas, and all through the cell,
Everyone was drinking tater water and was drunk as hell.
Their clothes were scattered from here to there;
Hoping they wouldn't get caught—but didn't really care.
They were sprawled all over the floor and the beds
While visions of hoe-squads danced in their heads.
And my buddy in his bunk, and I in mine,
Had just settled down—afraid of going back to the line—
When out in the hall there rose a loud tone,
I jumped from my bed to see what was going on.
Away to the door I flew like a flash,
Tripped over a locker and busted my ass!
The flashlights shining through the bars ahead
Made the night look like daytime instead.
When what to my sleepy eyes should appear
But Mr. Boren, grinning from ear to ear.
He had the troopers with him, stepping lively and quick.
I knew in a moment each one had a night stick.
More rapid than eagles his troopers they came,
And they whistled and shouted and called us bad names:
"Now bastards, now punks, now sons-of-bitches;
Get out of those beds, and put on your britches.

Get out those doors, and out in the halls;
Hurry up, damn it, or I'll kick you in the balls."
There was Mr. Lockhart, Major Fisher, too.
Terrell Don Hutto was there, drunk as hell,
Standing at the yard desk ringing a bell.
As I drew in my head, and was turning around,
Down the hall came an escapee who they had just found.
He was muddy as hell from his head to his feet,
His clothes were ragged and torn in the seat.
A pack of bloodhounds chased him down the hall,
And he looked like hell, and was about to fall.
His eyes were hollow, his face, how muddy;
His cheeks raw as hamburger, his nose bloody;
His mouth was busted and drawn up like a drum,
And where his teeth used to be, was nothing but gums.
He was skinny and thin and looked real silly;
I flinched in spite of myself when they hit him with a billy.
A swelling of his eye, and a knot on his head
Soon got me to wondering if he was alive or dead.
He spoke not a word, but jumped up from the floor;
Grabbed a trooper's 38 and ran for the door;
He shot some troopers, and bloodhounds a few;
He turned to Mr. Boren and said, "Screw you, too."
He grabbed his handkerchief to stop his bleeding nose,
And said, "When I leave here, nobody else goes."
He sprang out the front gate and into a police car;
No one knows which way he went or just how far;
But I heard him exclaim as he drove out of sight,
"Piss on you all, it's been a hell of a night."

KILLING TIME

Designed by Richard E. Rosenbaum. Composed by Vail-Ballou Press, Inc. in 10/12 Mergenthaler VIP Primer and Helvetica with display lines in Phototypositor Helvetica Extrabold Condensed. Camera, plates, and printing for duotone plates and text by Simpson/Milligan Printing Co., Inc. Printed by offset on Warren's Lustro Offset Enamel Dull, 70 pound basis. Bound by John H. Dekker and Sons, Inc. in Joanna Arrestox A, with stamping in All Purpose foil. Endpapers are Multicolor Antique Jet. Jackets printed by Simpson/Milligan.

Library of Congress Cataloging in Publication Data

(For library cataloging purposes only)

Jackson, Bruce.
  Killing time.

   1. Arkansas. Dept. of Correction. Cummins Unit. 2. Prisoners—Arkansas. I. Title.
HV9475.A93C854   365′.9767′823   77-6895
ISBN 0-8014-1101-7